AMERICA: UNDER ATTACK

By:
Allen Domelle

©Copyright 2018 Allen Domelle Ministries

ISBN: 978-0-9977894-4-7

All Scripture quotations are from the
Authorized King James Bible 1611

Visit our website at:
Oldpathsjournal.com
For more copies write:
Allen Domelle Ministries
PO Box 1595
Bethany, OK 73008
903.746.9632

Table of Contents

Foreword 1

Chapter 1
The Softening of the American Male 2

Chapter 2
The Homemaker Work Force
The Attack Against The Stay-at-Home Mom 11

Chapter 3
Cultural Attack Against the Scriptural Home 21

Chapter 4
Information Overload 32

Chapter 5
The Redefinition of Marriage 42

Chapter 6
The Social Acceptance Pressure 52

Chapter 7
Redefining Morality 61

Chapter 8
Judicial Injustice 71

Chapter 9
Entitlements
The Attack Against Work Ethics 80

Chapter 10
Tearing Down History 90

Chapter 11
Inclusive Tolerance
The Mega-Voice of Liberals 101

Chapter 12
Result-Focused 112

Chapter 13
Lowering the Bar 121

Chapter 14
Nanny State
The Battle for the Mind of Children 130

Chapter 15
I Am a Voice
The Attack Against Preaching 137

Chapter 16
 THE UNDERMINING OF AUTHORITY 145

Chapter 17
 THE CHURCH REDEFINED 155

Chapter 18
 GROOMING FOR THE WORLD 164

Chapter 19
 DON'T MOVE THE PULPIT 169

Chapter 20
 DRESSING DOWN DECENCY 175

Chapter 21
 ACTIONS WITH NO CONSEQUENCES 185

Chapter 22
 LEGACY DRIVEN SOCIETY 195

Chapter 23
 REDEFINING ROLE MODELS 204

Chapter 24
 THE DEVALUATION OF LIFE
 THE TURNING POINT IN AMERICAN MORALITY 212

Chapter 25
 DISTRACTION
 THE DEVIL'S TOOL TO DESTROY 218

Chapter 26
 IF MY PEOPLE 225

FOREWORD

It is with great pleasure that I write the foreword for this book. I personally read every word of this informative and needed book, and I do believe that everyone – both young and old – should read this to see what is wrong with our homes, our churches, and our country.

I pastored for almost 50 years. As I read this book, I thought of so many circumstances of when I dealt with families as to how I could have helped them with all the resources this book affords. Bro. Allen Domelle has taken pen in hand, not to condemn, but to warn and encourage us to what we must do to help the land heal. His goal is to help us independent, fundamental Baptist peoples, who seem to be less and less as the years go on.

I said that to say this; God has many times used the "few" who were dedicated to our Lord to defeat the "many." (Judges 7:12) In Acts 17:6, we see what happened in the span of fourteen years that started out with twelve people, then God added one hundred and twenty, then three thousand, etc. We have to get away from "It can't be done here" to *"I can do all things through Christ"* for the glory of God. I remind you; *"In the last days perilous* (grievous, dangerous) *times shall come."* (2 Timothy 3:1) The work continues!

Dr. B.G. Buchanan Sr.
Pastor Emeritus
Central Baptist Church
Baton Rouge, LA

CHAPTER 1

THE SOFTENING OF THE AMERICAN MALE

There used to be a day when men were not ashamed to be called men. If you insinuated that a man was anything less than a man, he would not cower to those who questioned his manhood and would quickly correct the matter. It used to be fighting words for a man to be called anything less than a man. Every boy had the image of a man as a rugged, tough individual who could do anything and stand up to anything.

Sadly, the softening of the American male has been Satan's agenda since he lost the battle against God in Heaven. Satan knows that he can destroy a society if he softens the male and sways them to leave their God-given roles. His agenda has been subtle as a serpent, but he has slowly chipped away at and destroyed the American male.

There were times when men would never be seen carrying anything that resembled a purse, but now we have men carrying man-purses known as murses. There was a day when men wouldn't be seen wearing pink because that was a sign of weakness; yet, today you have NFL players wearing pink on their uniforms to supposedly give attention to breast cancer awareness. I'm not saying a color defines a man, but I am pointing out that it has slowly come to the point where there are few differences between men and women.

There was a time when it was considered derogatory to call a man anything else other than a man. Today, men have their earrings and bracelets, are not afraid to be called metrosexual, and many don't even know what it is like to get their hands dirty. In years past, these things were not the norm; yet, today you are looked down upon if you don't consider them normal.

Hollywood created its agenda to soften the American male through its programming that portrays men as bumbling idiots who can't make a decision or do anything right. The constant barrage of attacks against strong male leadership has caused many to draw back or apologize for simply doing what men are supposed to do. Hollywood has an agenda with these barrage of attacks, and that agenda is anti-God.

The softening of the American male has started in the leadership of the home, church and society. If men stop acting like men, it affects the strength of the home. If you make the homes weak, you will weaken the church and its ability to reach the lost for Jesus Christ. When the church is weak, society will turn into chaos. The softening of the American male is a concerted effort to destroy our Christian society.

Satan knows exactly what he is doing by attempting to soften the American male. He knows that the softening of the male is a way to get people to turn to godless activity. Man was made in the image of God, and if Satan can devalue the male image, he can cause individuals to lose confidence in God.

When you look at Jesus Christ in the Scriptures, you will find that His manhood was never questioned. The woman at the well described Jesus by saying, *"Come, **see a man**, which told me all things that ever I did: is not this the Christ?"* (John 4:29) The Apostle Paul defined Jesus in 1 Timothy 2:5, *"For there is one God, and one mediator between God and men, **the man Christ Jesus**;"* In both instances, Jesus was not defined as a soft male with long hair as the average artist rendition of Jesus portrays; instead, Jesus was indisputably defined as a man. There was no question as to the manhood of Jesus Christ.

If we are going to keep our nation strong, we are going to have to raise young boys to be men. If our nation is to continue to be a Christian nation, the men of our nation, especially the Christian men, are going to have to act like a man according to the Scriptures. The Scriptures give several characteristics and responsibilities of the man.

1. Man was made to conquer.

Since the beginning of creation, God made man to have the need to conquer something every day. Genesis 1:26-27 says, *"And God said, Let us make man in our image, after our likeness: and let them have dominion over the fish of the sea, and over the fowl of the air, and over the cattle, and over all the earth, and over every creeping thing that creepeth upon the earth. So God created man in his own image, in the image of God created he him; male and female created he them."* The psalmist makes clear what God wants a man to do when it says, *"What is man, that thou art mindful of him? and the son of man, that thou visitest him? For thou hast made him a little lower than the angels, and hast crowned him with glory and honour. Thou madest him to have dominion over the works of thy hands; thou hast put all things under his feet:"*

You will notice that man was to have *"dominion"* over God's creation. If you are going to have dominion over something, you are going to have to conquer it. At the end of each day, a man must have conquered something to feel complete. If a man doesn't conquer something throughout the day, he will be frustrated at the end of each day.

When I was a boy, my friend and I used to set up plastic army men as if we were engaged in battle against them. We took our bb guns and shot each one of those "attacking" us, and when all was said and done, we won the war. That was part of the spirit that God put in men to conquer something.

A man may not shoot plastic army men every day, but they must conquer something every day. At the day's end, a man needs to know that they have completed something. Men need to be completers because men were made to conquer. If a man is going to be who he is scripturally supposed to be, he will need to finish or conquer something each day.

2. Man was made to work.

Genesis 1:28 says, *"And God blessed them, and God said unto them, Be fruitful, and multiply, and replenish the earth, and subdue it: and have dominion over the fish of the sea, and over the fowl of the air, and over every living thing that moveth upon the earth."* You will notice that the first thing that God commanded man to do was to work. It is work to subdue the Earth. Genesis 3:19 says, *"In the sweat of thy face shalt thou eat bread, till thou return unto the ground; for out of it wast thou taken: for dust thou art, and unto dust shalt thou return."* It is part of man's nature to work and sweat.

One thing every mother must be careful of is discouraging her boy from getting sweaty and dirty. It is part of the male's makeup for the boy to get dirty and sweaty; it prepares them to work. It is good for a boy to go work with his dad. I always enjoy watching men who take their boys to work with them because that is what my father did with me. It teaches the boy that part of being a man is working. It helps that boy to get the good feeling at the end of the day that working gives.

One thing this culture has tried to do is make it normal for man to stay home while the woman works. This is a sinful mentality that goes directly against the Word of God. Man will not be who he is supposed to be without working, and let me add, working hard.

3. Man is made to be the bread winner.

One of the things this society has done to soften the American male is to make it sound normal for men to be at-home-mommies, whatever that is. It is the man's responsibility to pay the bills and earn the money to make sure everything in the home is cared for. 1 Timothy 5:8 says, *"But if any provide not for his own, and specially for those of his own house, he hath denied the faith, and is worse than an infidel."* You will notice God says, *"his own."* This is a masculine term. In other words, God wants the man to be the one to provide for the house.

You must not settle for society's attack against the man being the breadwinner of the home. There is nothing wrong with the man taking ownership of his responsibility to pay the bills. A real man will want to be the one who pays the bills and will not look for handouts from others. He realizes his responsibility is to care for the responsibilities of his home and family.

4. Man was made to be different from the woman.

Men and women are different, in spite of how society has tried to attack these differences. Genesis 1:27 makes this difference clear when it says, *"So God created man in his own image, in the image of God created he him; male and female created he them."* I know this goes in the face of our modern culture, but men are different from women, and they should act, talk and dress differently.

There is nothing wrong with a man acknowledging that he is a stronger vessel than the lady. The man should know that he is to protect the lady. The man should open the door for the lady, fix the things around the house, be sure that he takes care of all the things of a physical nature that need to be maintained. Don't let modern society's push to soften the American male cause you to think that being different from the woman is inferior. It is not inferior; it is scriptural.

5. Man is to be the decision-maker.

One of the ways that society has tried to soften the American male is through displaying man's inability to make decisions. If you watch the advertisements on television, you would think that man has no common sense and can only survive because of a woman. This is no doubt the attempt of Satan to make men step back from their responsibility of being the decision-maker.

Numbers 30:14 says, *"But if her husband altogether hold his peace at her from day to day; then he establisheth all her vows, or all her bonds, which are upon her: he confirmeth them, because he held his peace at her in the day that he heard them."* This verse shows how the husband, or man, is to be the final decision-maker on every decision. According to the Scriptures, a husband validates or invalidates his wife's or daughter's decision.

I know this directly contradicts the politically correct agenda, but it is a man's responsibility to make decisions. Men shouldn't take second seat to the decisions in the home and church. Every man should be actively involved in the decisions, and stop being passive about who makes the final decision. Sin was the result of Abram taking a passive role in the decision making of his home. I'm not saying that a lady cannot help in the decision-making process, but what I am saying is that the man needs to make the final decision in his home and in society.

6. Men are to be masculine.

One of the things that truly bothers me in our modern day culture is the effeminate tendencies of many men. 1 Corinthians 6:9-10 shows God's displeasure toward effeminate men when it says, *"Know ye not that the unrighteous shall not inherit the kingdom of God? Be not* deceived: neither fornicators, nor idolaters, nor adulterers, nor effeminate, nor abusers of themselves with mankind, Nor thieves, nor covetous, nor drunkards, nor revilers, nor extortioners, shall inherit the kingdom of God."

No man should ever act, walk or talk like a woman. Men who are effeminate in nature are in direct disobedience to God. Men are not born effeminate, but they are trained to be effeminate. They are trained to be effeminate when they are allowed to whine when they are hurt, to stay in the home instead of going outside, or protected from any circumstance that could cause them a little physical pain.

If you want to keep your boys from having effeminate tendencies, you would be wise to get them involved in manly activities. It doesn't hurt for boys to go hunting, play physical sports, physically labor, and participate in manly activities. Effeminate boys are groomed by someone to act more like a woman than a man. If a boy is raised around men, you will find him to have manly tendencies.

7. Men are to lead.

Leading is not being placed in a position of leadership as much as it is taking charge of situations to be sure they are done right. Ephesians 5:23 says, *"For the husband is the head of the wife, even as Christ is the head of the church: and he is the saviour of the body."* The head is the leader. In other words, men see something that needs to get done, and they step up and lead.

One of the things that is killing our churches is the lack of male leadership. The average church survives because the ladies are the ones who have stepped up and made sure the duties of the church are completed. It is sad to watch the average man sit in the background and watch his wife do all the work. Men should be the leaders in the home, church and society. They should be the first to fill the positions that are needed to keep the church aggressively reaching their community. Softened men won't fill positions because they are not strong enough to handle the criticism. A scriptural man will take the lead in the home and church, and won't be afraid to be criticized because that comes with leadership.

8. Man is to live in the image of God.

Man was created in God's image; this means a man should emulate God. A real man is going to live a holy life. He will keep his mind pure and his body from fornication or adultery. He will possess his vessel with character so that God's image can be seen through his life. Manliness is more than having a rugged personality or a muscle-bound body, though there is nothing wrong with either, but manliness is a man who lives his life in the holy image that God made man to be.

These eight areas are what God expects from men. If you want to soften the American male, take each of these areas away from him and you will find a soft man who displeases His God. My friend, let's be careful about not letting Satan's attack to soften the male enter the thresholds of our homes. It is high time every man takes inventory of who he is and be sure that he becomes that strong individual who is manly, holy and living in the image of God.

CHAPTER 2

THE HOMEMAKER WORK FORCE
THE ATTACK AGAINST THE STAY-AT-HOME MOM

Several years ago when my wife and I went to purchase our first home, we went to the bank to fill out an application to see if the bank would approve us for a loan. The lady who was helping us with this application began to ask me all the personal questions needed from me to get the application approved.

After she was done gathering my information, she turned to my wife and began asking her the personal information needed to complete the application. When she got to the part of the application where you give your employment details, she asked my wife where she worked. My wife responded that she was a stay-at-home mom, or homemaker, whichever she wanted to put on the application. You would have thought my wife had slapped this woman in the face with this response. The lady asked my wife if there was anything she did outside the home where she earned money. Again, my wife responded that she was a homemaker and that she helped to raise our daughter at home while I was gone.

The sad part about this woman's response is that she thought my wife was being repressed by a husband who wouldn't let her work. However, if you were to ask my wife if it ever bothered her to be a homemaker, she would cheerfully respond that she is thrilled to have a husband who understands his role of being the breadwinner, which allows her to fulfill her role of being a homemaker. In all the years that my wife and I have been married, I can't recall one time when she complained about not working outside the home. In fact, the opposite has been true of my wife. She has always appreciated that I have made it possible for her to fulfill her scriptural role as a wife and mother.

For years, society has tried to attack the stay-at-home mom who understands her role in the home. Just like television has portrayed men as bumbling idiots, it has also portrayed ladies who desire to be a homemaker as out-of-touch with modern culture, or repressed by an oppressive husband. It is again an attack against the scriptural model of what God wants a lady to be.

Several things have contributed to the loss of the stay-at-home wife and mother. One of the ways society has attacked the homemaker is by trying to masculinize the lady. Instead of keeping the lady feminine, society has championed the equality of the sexes, which is a direct contradiction of the Scriptures. Genesis 1:27 reminds us of the difference between men and women when it says, *"So God created man in his own image, in the image of God created he him; male and female created he them."*

Today we have women who are as crude in language and appearance as you would expect from a man. Women talk as vulgar as a drunken sailor. Instead of a woman looking like a lady, they have tattoos all over their body, which demeans their femininity. Sports leagues now exist for women which is another attack against the homemaker. (Who would have ever thought that women's boxing would be something our society would embrace?) Women have become loud, boisterous and bossy. Sadly, more women desire a career more than having children and being a keeper at home. All of this is an attack against God's plan for women to be at home which is essential for the home to be what the LORD intended for it to be.

Moreover, the cost of living has also contributed to the attack against the stay-at-home wife and mother. It is almost impossible in some parts of America for a man to earn enough money just to pay the mortgage. Whether or not this is part of society's plan, I can say that it is part of Satan's plan to pull the lady out of the home. He knows that if the lady is not in the home, the home will become dysfunctional, children will become unruly, and marriages will be destroyed.

I know what I have written in this chapter is not popular in our day, but all you have to do is look at where society has gone since World War II when women were forced to go to the factories and work because the men were overseas fighting for our freedoms. Since the women have left the home, the divorce rate has risen, children are becoming more and more rebellious, and the feminine lady has become a rarity in our society.

If we are going to turn these things around, we are going to have to get our ladies to get back to understanding their scriptural roles. It will have to start by teaching young girls their proper roles, and also warn them of society's attack against the homemaker. When looking through the Scriptures, there are eleven characteristics and responsibilities a lady is to have and perform. In each of these characteristics or responsibilities, Satan's desire is to keep the lady from acting like this or from fulfilling their role. Let me share with you these eleven characteristics or responsibilities.

1. The woman is to be a help to the man.

From the beginning of creation, God intended for the lady to be a help to her husband. Genesis 2:18 says, *"And the LORD God said, It is not good that the man should be alone; I will make him an help meet for him."* God never intended for the lady to lead the man; instead, He intended for her to help complete her husband, being that cheerleader and caretaker at home to help her husband reach his God-given potential.

1 Corinthians 11:9 reminds us, *"Neither was the man created for the woman; but the woman for the man."* I know to modern society this verse is politically incorrect, but the lady will always feel like she is missing out on something until she becomes a help meet for her husband. God never intended for a lady to have the "help me" mentality that so many women have today, but He intended for her to be the *"help meet"* for her husband. I'm very thankful for a wife who has always filled this role in our home by making sure my clothes are always clean, meals are provided, and any need I have is met. Ladies, you will never regret being the help meet for your husband when you see him reach his God-given potential because of your of help.

2. She is to be the keeper of the home.

When God talks about the responsibility of the woman, He says in Titus 2:5, *"To be discreet, chaste, keepers at home..."*

I can see the modern-day feminist rolling her eyes and already beginning to say that I am a male chauvinist. You can label as you wish; however, you can't deny that God's Word commands the lady to be a keeper *"at home."*

This carries two connotations. First, the lady is to be sure the home is kept clean and tidy. I'm thankful that for all these years my wife has always made sure our home is clean. The second connotation is that the lady is to guard the home against outside influences. A lady's intuition can protect the home tremendously from outside influences that can harm the marriage and children. If a lady is out building her career, she won't see those dangerous influences that are creeping in to destroy her home.

3. She is to be the key role in rearing the children.

The stay-at-home mom plays a great role in rearing the children. Proverbs 31:28 shows this when it says about the mother, *"Her children arise up, and call her blessed; her husband also, and he praiseth her."* Proverbs 29:15 shows the importance of the lady staying at home to rear the children when it says, *"The rod and reproof give wisdom: but a child left to himself bringeth his mother to shame."*

Children need their mother, not a babysitter or a child-care center. Nobody can meet the needs of a child like their mother. One of the reasons so many children have problems today can be traced back to the fact that mom wasn't available to help them through their difficulties, and to instill the proper character traits they need to become the individual God wants them to be.

4. She is to be chaste.

One of the ways that Satan has attacked the home is through ladies interaction with men in the workplace. Satan uses the everyday camaraderie at the workplace between men and women to tempt them with adultery. All it takes is for a man or woman to see how someone at work treats them "so much better" than their spouse. The temptation begins, and before they realize how far they have allowed their mind and emotions to go, they find themselves in an adulterous affair that would have never happened had the lady been the homemaker as God intended.

Titus 2:5 reminds us that the lady is to be *"chaste."* The word *"chaste"* is talking about being pure from any illicit activities with the opposite gender. It also means that a lady is to be pure in her language. Most women pick up the vulgar, off-color conversations and words from the world. If she stays home, she will be able to keep herself from talking in such a crude manner. Moreover, a lady has a much higher chance of being pure if she fulfills her God-given role of being a homemaker.

5. She is to follow her husband's leadership.

One of the things the feminist agenda has pushed is that the lady should not submit to the "leadership of her husband." Whether or not society likes it, God still gives the leadership role to the husband. God says in Titus 2:5, *"To be discreet, chaste, keepers at home, good, obedient to their own husbands…"* Since the beginning, God intended the lady to follow her husband's leadership. Genesis 3:16 reminds us of this when it says, *"…thy desire shall be to thy husband,*

and he shall rule over thee." It may not be politically correct, but it is scripturally correct for a lady to follow her husband's leadership. Somebody has to be in charge and make the final decision. God chose the husband to be the one to make the final decision. If you don't like the idea of the man being the final decision-maker, you need to take it up with God because He is the one who gave this responsibility to the man.

6. She is to be a teacher to those who are younger.

One reason a lady needs to be a homemaker is because somebody needs to teach the children. Titus 2:4 says, *"That they may teach the young women to be sober, to love their husbands, to love their children,"* In most homes, you will find that the mother has instilled the character traits in the children. This is a normal tendency, especially in the homes where the mother is a homemaker.

If you allow the daycare center to instill character in your children, you will find your children will miss what you know they need. Though daycare workers have great intentions, there is no way they will know what your children need because they are not the parent. God gave you your children because He knew you would be the best trainer for them. Satan will tempt the lady to go into the work force so that he can steal the mind of the child. A child has a better chance of turning out right for the LORD if their mother is at home rearing them.

7. She is to be meek and quiet in spirit.

One of the characteristics of many women today is their boisterous and loud talk. There used to be a time when I was young when every lady carried herself in a quiet manner, and she never wanted to bring attention to herself with her loud talk or over-the-top emotions.

God says about the lady in 1 Peter 3:4, *"But let it be the hidden man of the heart, in that which is not corruptible, even the ornament of a meek and quiet spirit, which is in the sight of God of great price."* The lady is supposed to have a *"meek and quiet spirit."* This does not mean that she can't talk, but it means that she doesn't bring attention to herself by how loud she is or how outrageous she acts. Though society may portray this as normal, it is unscriptural and harmful to a lady's testimony.

God shows what He thinks about this loud spirit in Proverbs 7:11 when He says, *"She is loud and stubborn; her feet abide not in her house;"* This verse is talking about the characteristics of the strange woman. If a lady has the meek and quiet spirit that God wants her to have, it will help to keep temptation away from her marriage.

8. She is to be feminine in nature.

Proverbs 21:9 says, *"It is better to dwell in a corner of the housetop, than with a brawling woman in a wide house."* The *"brawling woman"* is the woman who thinks she is a man. She wants to act like a man, work like a man, and participate in the same activities of a man. Satan's attack against the feminine nature of the lady has come through women's athletics, careers and equal rights movement that have pushed that a woman is just as capable of doing all the same things physically that a man can do.

My friend, this is simply absurd. God says in 1 Peter 3:7, *"Likewise, ye husbands, dwell with them according to knowledge, giving honour unto the wife, as unto the weaker vessel…"* According to God's Word, a lady is not physically as strong as the man. God says that she is the *"weaker vessel."* There is nothing wrong with understanding that a lady cannot do what a man can do. As long as we cower to Satan's message that the lady can do anything a man can do, we will continue to see homes destroyed, society weakened, and God's order for leadership crumble.

9. She is to be prudent and wise in word.

One of the wisest and perceptive people I know is my wife. Because she has embraced God's role for the lady in her life, I believe she has so much more insight than the average lady who rebels against God's role. My wife has given me a lot of good advice because of her wisdom. Her wisdom has given her the instinct to see things before I have seen them. My wife is not weak because she chooses to follow, but her wisdom and perception have grown because the LORD has honored her obedience to His Word.

Many may think that this chapter is demeaning to the lady, but what they don't understand is that God gives extra wisdom to the lady who fulfills her God-given role. Proverbs 31:26 says, *"She openeth her mouth with wisdom…"* If a lady embraces the role that God wants her to be, she will find that He will fill *"her mouth with wisdom."* Some of the wisest people I have been around are ladies who learned God's wisdom by embracing their role as a homemaker.

10. She is to care for her husband's personal needs.

Though I mentioned this in a previous point in this chapter, let me point out that the role of the lady is to be sure her husband's needs are met. Proverbs 31:11 says, *"The heart of her husband doth safely trust in her, so that he shall have no need of spoil."* Ladies, your husband should never have to ask you to care for the needs of the home or his personal need. Your responsibility is to be sure that he has *"no need of spoil."*

11. She is to live in the fear of God.

One of the greatest attributes a lady can have is a fear of God. Proverbs 31:30 says about the virtuous woman, *"Favour is deceitful, and beauty is vain: but a woman that feareth the LORD, she shall be praised."* The greatest beauty a lady can have is living in the fear of God. This doesn't mean she is constantly living in trepidation of what God will do to her, but it means that she respects God and what He can do for her with His power if she fills her God-given role. Though there is nothing wrong with trying to look pretty for your husband, the best way to keep your beauty is by fearing the LORD.

I know this chapter is politically incorrect, but our society has attacked the stay-at-home wife and mother to the point that many ladies are ashamed to say that is what they do. Never be ashamed of being a homemaker. If anything, you should be honored that you can live such a life. Don't allow the voices of society to shame you into forsaking your God-given role. Embrace it and accept it, because you will be glad you did when you are married happily for many years, and when you see your children serving the LORD.

CHAPTER 3

CULTURAL ATTACK AGAINST THE SCRIPTURAL HOME

The best way to destroy a society is to destroy the home. Satan knows that in order to destroy the local church and our American society that he must do so through a cultural attack against the scriptural home. A church or society is only as strong as the home. If you weaken the home, you weaken society. Most of our present societal problems can be traced directly back to dysfunctional homes.

Dysfunctional homes produce weak neighborhoods. When you look at the neighborhoods where crime is rampant, you can look at the strength of the family units and discover that many of those children have been reared in single-parent households. You could drastically lower the crime in troubled neighborhoods if the homes were scripturally sound.

Dysfunctional homes give place to disrespect of authority. The reason authority is under attack is because scriptural authority has not been established in the home units. Satan knows that he can undermine authority if he can attack the scriptural authority in the home.

Dysfunctional homes hinder children from growing up in the nurture and admonition of the LORD. When a child grows up with both parents teaching and enforcing the Scriptures, you will find children moving into their adult years with a better chance of loving the LORD and a desire to serve Him as well as a healthy respect for authority.

Dysfunctional homes hinder children from fully developing into the image of God. The home should mirror God. When Satan attacks the home through a corrupt culture, he is doing so to keep children from learning about God and His guidelines for how a home should function.

Dysfunctional homes contribute to the rise in crime, the lowering of church attendance, the demise of the roles of the male and female, and the illegitimacy and the loss of purity among our youth. When homes function according to God's design, you will find children more likely keeping the laws, going to church, understanding and fulfilling their gender roles, and they will have a desire to stay pure until the day of marriage.

Satan attacks the scriptural home through culture. Our American culture is sadly being dictated by wicked Hollywood celebrities, worldly music icons, sports figures, and liberal teachers. Ephesians 2:2 shows us that Satan controls culture when it says, *"Wherein in time past ye walked according to the course of this world, according to **the prince of the power of the air**, the spirit that now worketh in the children of disobedience:"* We must understand that the home is constantly under attack because the strength of the church and society depend upon its strength. If Satan can use the filthy, vulgar and ungodly culture to infiltrate the homes and destroy them, he can then destroy the Christian society upon which America was founded.

Satan's attack against the scriptural home started in the Book of Genesis. If you want to see the effects of dysfunctional homes on society, look no further than how culture affected the families in the Book of Genesis. Every problem we find in the Book of Genesis can be traced back to some dysfunction in the home. Satan used culture to influence these homes.

It all started in the Garden of Eden when Satan filled the serpent and affected the culture in which Adam and Eve lived. The first thing that Satan did to attack the home was to attack the roles of authority which God established. Genesis 3:1 says, *"Now the serpent was more subtil than any beast of the field which the LORD God had made. And he said unto the woman, Yea, hath God said, Ye shall not eat of every tree of the garden?"* Satan got Eve to take the leading role in the home, which led to sin entering into the world. Had Eve not allowed the culture of the serpent to influence her and instead gone to her husband for leadership, sin would not have entered into the world.

Abram and Sarai succumbed to Satan's attack against their home by allowing the culture that surrounded them to influence their desire for a child in a sinful manner. Genesis 16:2 shows the attack against the scriptural home when it says, *"And Sarai said unto Abram, Behold now, the LORD hath restrained me from bearing: I pray thee, go in unto my maid; it may be that I may obtain children by her. And Abram hearkened to the voice of Sarai."* Abram should have told his wife that they didn't live like the sinful culture around them because they represented a different culture and that culture was God's. Sadly, they succumbed, and the yielding to the pressure of their culture led to a dysfunctional home with an illegitimate child.

Isaac and Rebekah succumbed to Satan's attack against their home by each parent having their favorite child, which resulted in a home filled with deceit. Jacob's home was also dysfunctional by marrying multiple wives and allowing the gods of the world to influence the culture of his home. Twice Jacob told his family to put away the strange gods. It is no wonder that his home was so dysfunctional.

Your home is continually under attack by today's culture. You must realize that Satan will do everything he can to get the present-day culture to influence your home so that it will be destroyed. If we are going to fight back against the cultural attack against the scriptural home, we must be sure to pattern our homes according to God's design. Let me show you eleven ways that God wants the home to function.

1. God's order for the family is marriage before children.

To understand God's order, all you have to do is go back to the original family and see how God started it. Genesis 1:28 says, *"And God blessed them, and God said unto them, Be fruitful, and multiply, and replenish the earth…"* Notice that it was after God blessed Adam and Eve in marriage that He commanded them to *"multiply, and replenish the earth."* God's order is marriage before children.

God shows His disdain for this order being reversed in Hebrews 13:4 when He says, *"Marriage is honourable in all, and the bed undefiled: but whoremongers and adulterers God will judge."* This verse makes it clear that God is against the cultural mentality that a man and woman live together to determine whether they are compatible. Any intimacy outside of the boundaries of marriage is wrong. God's order of marriage before children is what keeps the home functioning according to God's design. When you keep this order right, you will find it easier to establish a scriptural home.

2. Divorce is never an option.

Society has made it normal for people to get divorced, but God has made it clear that divorce should never be an option. Romans 7:2-3 says, *"For the woman which hath an husband is bound by the law to her husband so long as he liveth; but if the husband be dead, she is loosed from the law of her husband. So then if, while her husband liveth, she be married to another man, she shall be called an adulteress: but if her husband be dead, she is free from that law; so that she is no adulteress, though she be married to another man."* If the woman is bound to the husband till he dies, that means that the man is also bound to his wife until she dies.

Many people have succumbed to the cultural attack against the home through divorce by saying that the Scriptures allows it. Matthew 19:8 says, *"He saith unto them, Moses because of the hardness of your hearts suffered you to put away your wives: but from the beginning it was not so."* Notice that it was the "hardness" of the hearts that caused people to get divorced. In other words, it doesn't matter what the spouse who does wrong does to get right, a hard heart never accepts it. God makes it clear in this verse that *"from the beginning"* He never intended for divorce to be an option. The best way to fight the cultural attack against the home is for each spouse to determine to work through every problem no matter how difficult it may be.

3. God is the chief authority of the home.

1 Corinthians 11:3 says, *"But I would have you know, that the head of every man is Christ; and the head of the woman is the man; and the head of Christ is God."* If a home is going to be what it ought to be, Christ is going to have to be the head of that home. The home must not be a place that we work God into, but it must be a place where Christ is the central focus of all that we do. A scriptural home will be a place where our opinions don't matter. When everyone in the home looks to the Scriptures for what they are to do, you are ultimately defeating the cultural attack against your home. Culture dictates that everyone does what they want to do; whereas, the Scriptures teach that Christ must dictate the actions and beliefs of the home. When Christ is the chief authority of the home, every other problem will be quickly solved.

4. The husband is to be the head of the home.

Ephesians 5:23 says, *"For the husband is the head of the wife, even as Christ is the head of the church..."* Culture constantly attacks God's structure of authority in the home because if God's structure of authority is defeated, Christ will ultimately not be the chief authority in the home.

5. The wife is to submit to her husband's leadership.

It is interesting that before God commanded the husband to be the *"head of the wife,"* that He commanded the wife to submit to her husband's leadership. Ephesians 5:22 says, *"Wives, submit yourselves unto your own husbands, as unto the Lord."* I know that society has dictated this scriptural structure as archaic and out-of-touch with modern culture, but the Scriptures always trump culture. Somebody has to be the head of the home, which means that the one who is not the head must submit to the leadership of the head. Because God made the man the *"head of the wife,"* she must submit if the home is going to function according to God's design. If a wife truly loves her husband and children, she will obey this command to submit to her husband's leadership.

This doesn't mean that the man can do whatever he wants. A scriptural husband will love his wife. Ephesians 5:25 says, *"Husbands, love your wives, even as Christ also loved the church, and gave himself for it;"* If a husband loves his wife, he will give himself to her. In other words, he doesn't run over his wife; rather, he will be sure to take her thoughts into consideration when he makes the final decision.

6. Children are to obey their parents.

Ephesians 6:1 says, *"Children, obey your parents in the Lord: for this is right."* One of the ways culture has attacked the scriptural home is to get the parents to make everything revolve around the children. The Scriptures make it clear that children live in their parent's world not vice versa. The home should not be a place where the children lead the parents. Too many parents allow their children to dictate what they do instead of the parents parenting and telling the children how they are going to live.

Joshua was not only a great leader, but he was a great parent. He said in Joshua 24:15, *"...as for me and my house, we will serve the LORD."* You will notice that Joshua didn't consult his children as to whether they were going to serve the LORD; rather, he told them that they were going to serve the LORD. Parents, it is your job to decide according to the Scriptures what is allowed in your home. Stop asking your children what they want to do, and show them from the Scriptures what they are to believe and do.

You will find that if the authority structure for the husband and wife is followed, it will be much easier for the children to obey their parents. However, if children see their parents faltering in their responsibilities in the home, they will take advantage of this weakness and drive a wedge between their parents. Let me encourage every parent to stop trying to be a friend to your children and be their parent. God never said that you are to be their friend, but He did say that you are to *"bring them up in the nurture and admonition of the Lord."* (Ephesians 6:4)

7. Family's should serve the LORD together.

Joshua didn't say that he and his wife were going to serve the LORD, but he said that his *"house"* was going to serve the LORD. One of Pharaoh's compromises he offered Moses was to let the parents go sacrifice, but leave the children in Egypt. My friend, serving the LORD together is the best family time you can have. Some of the best times I have had with my daughter have been when we served the LORD together. Make serving the LORD a highlight of your family. Find ministries in your church where you can do things together as a family. This will not only create great memories, but it will strengthen the structure of your home.

8. Children are to be reared to fulfill God's purpose for their lives.

Psalm 127:3 says, *"Lo, children are an heritage of the LORD: and the fruit of the womb is his reward."* The word "heritage" is the same word we use for an estate or possessions. In other words, the Scriptures teach that children belong to God. If you rear your children to fulfill your desires, you will find that your children will become selfish and spoiled. It should never be about what we want or what they want because your children belong to the LORD. The responsibility of the parent is to help their children to learn what God wants them to do with their life.

Parents, stop trying to relive your childhood through your children. Your job as a parent is not to try to fulfill your dreams through your children of what you feel you missed out on in your childhood. Likewise, you are not to rear your children to take over the family business. You are to find what God placed them on this Earth to do, and help rear them in such a manner that their sole desire is to fulfill His purpose for their life, even if that means they must move away.

9. Grandparents are to support the authority of their children.

Proverbs 17:6 is a grandparents verse when it says, *"Children's children are the crown of old men; and the glory of children are their fathers."* There is nothing that will brighten the eyes of a person than to hear them proudly talk about their grandchildren. Every parent understands the wonder as to why their parents didn't treat them the same way they treat their grandchildren. The reason is because grandchildren *"are the crown of old men."*

However, this doesn't mean that the grandparents are to spoil their grandchildren. Just because you can send them home doesn't mean you should let your grandchildren do what they want to do. If you want your grandchildren to continue to be your crown, you had better support the parent's authority. Romans 13:1 still says, *"Let every soul be subject unto the higher powers…"* The authority of the child is their parent, and for a grandparent not to enforce the rules of the parents is teaching the grandchildren that the rules of their parents are not important. Moreover, nowhere do the Scriptures teach that the grandparents are a greater authority than the parents over their grandchildren. God told children to obey their parents, which means that grandparents should support the parental authority of their grandchildren.

10. Morality and decency are paramount to a godly home.

Leviticus 18:7 teaches the importance of decency in the home when it says, *"The nakedness of thy father, or the nakedness of thy mother, shalt thou not uncover: she is thy mother; thou shalt not uncover her nakedness."* God reinforces the importance of decency between siblings in verse 9 by saying, *"The nakedness of thy sister, the daughter of thy father, or daughter of thy mother, whether she be born at home, or born abroad, even their nakedness thou shalt not uncover."*

Dressing decently around the home is essential to keeping your home pure. Just because you are family doesn't give you a right to be indecent in front of each other. Brothers and sisters should never be allowed to bathe together. Everyone in the home should be fully dressed whenever they leave the bedroom. If you want to keep immorality from destroying your home, you had better demand that everyone is dressed decently at all times.

11. God's Word must be the central control for a functional, godly home.

2 Timothy 3:15 says, *"And that from a child thou hast known the holy scriptures, which are able to make thee wise unto salvation through faith which is in Christ Jesus."* The best way to fight the cultural attack against your home is to keep the Scriptures as the central focus of belief and practice in your home. The importance of everyone in the home reading the Scriptures daily can never be over emphasized. One of the best ways to keep everyone in the Scriptures daily is by having family devotions. When you make the Scriptures your focus for belief and practice, you will find that your children will look at societal culture as abnormal.

Always keep in mind that Satan will do everything in his power to attack your home. My friend, you can't get out of living in the world, but you can keep the world from pushing its culture into your home. If you want to have a strong and happy home, you are going to have to follow God's pattern for the home. God designed the family unit, and He knows what is best for the family and how to create a happy and peaceful atmosphere in the home for all to enjoy.

Chapter 4

INFORMATION OVERLOAD

We live in a technological age. The ability to get information at a moments notice is at the tips of our fingers. With the 24-hour news media, social media and the internet, it is easy for anyone to get overloaded with information. The sad part is that, most of the time, the information we receive through these outlets is not glorifying to God, nor is it going to build a Christ-like spirit.

When I was a boy, it was a whole lot simpler to control the information of life. When I was young, there were no 24-hour news channels. As a boy, most of the news we got came from the radio because most people didn't have televisions in their home. By the time I was a teenager, most people had televisions, but you still only got the news once, or at the most, twice a day. You didn't leave the television on all day as background noise because you only had a few channels you could get, and those channels didn't play anything that a Christian should watch during the daytime. By the time I graduated from high school, you could watch the news at 6 PM, and if you stayed up late enough, you could watch the 11 PM news which was followed by a late-night national news. The news media wasn't a controlling factor in most people's lives. Most people chose what news they received by reading the paper instead of watching the news, but that has changed tremendously since the 24-hour cable news networks came into existence.

Likewise, social media didn't exist when I was a teenager. There were no group chats, private messengers, or social media platforms for young people to get their minds corrupted from the filth that often comes through these mediums. Information was much easier to keep under control because everyone didn't have a smartphone where they could constantly access their social media sites or browse the internet. Keeping the wrong information away from the youth, and even the adults, was much easier when these things were not a part of our lives.

Moreover, when I was a boy, the plethora of cable television networks wasn't a part of anyone's life. Parents didn't have to worry about what their children were watching because there wasn't anything to watch. I'm not saying that the youth couldn't get bad information back in the day, but I am saying that it wasn't as accessible as it is today.

Satan has always had his way of getting the wrong information to people; it is just that it is much easier to get to that wrong information today. Ephesians 2:2 shows us why Satan seems to rule the information world when it says, *"Wherein in time past ye walked according to the course of this world, according to the **prince of the power of the air**, the spirit that now worketh in the children of disobedience:"* Satan is a master at overloading the Christian with the wrong information, and that information has ruined many minds, marriages and lives.

The information overload we experience today is because of too many voices we allow in our lives. Satan started overloading God's people with information all the way back in the Garden of Eden by putting another voice in Eve's life. Genesis 3:1 says, *"Now the serpent was more subtil than any beast of the field which the LORD God had made. And he said unto the woman..."* Before this time, the only voices Eve had in her life was her husband's and God's. It was much easier for Eve to do right when she wasn't overloaded with information coming from all the different voices, but once there came another voice in her life it caused her to have to evaluate all that God had told her.

Satan gave Eve false information when he asked, *"...Yea, hath God said, Ye shall not eat of every tree of the garden?"* Because Eve had another voice in her life, she felt she had to answer the voice which created questions and doubt in her mind. She said in verses 2-3, *"...We may eat of the fruit of the trees of the garden: But of the fruit of the tree which is in the midst of the garden, God hath said, Ye shall not eat of it, neither shall ye touch it, lest ye die."* Eve's answer was not one of confidence, but a defensive one in hopes that the extra voice would be silenced, but it wasn't. Once the Christian responds to Satan's false information, he continues until the Christian is overloaded and surrenders to the voices in their life. Had Eve controlled the information in her life, she would have never committed the first sin.

The problem with all of the mediums of information that are available today is that there is no way to control them. Israel became a society much like we are today where it had no king to control what they did; thus, they did what they thought was right. Judges 21:25 says, *"In those days there was no king in Israel: every man did that which was right in his own eyes."* Just like Israel had no king to dictate what they should do, many people today have no governor which controls the information they receive. The result is an information overload which often is not true; thus, it causes people to believe the lies as truth. Most of the information we receive cannot be validated, and because of the plethora of false information which Satan allows to cross your screens, many fall trap for the lies, and it changes the attitudes of Christians and also the manner in which many serve the LORD.

If you don't want to fall for the lies Satan propagates through the media airwaves, whether it is social media, news media or the internet, you are going to have to learn how to control your information. Let me give you several statements and helps on how to control the information overload.

1. Satan is battling for your mind.

The biggest battleground for the Christian is their mind. That is why God says in 2 Corinthians 10:5, *"Casting down **imaginations**, and every high thing that exalteth itself against the knowledge of God, and **bringing into captivity every thought** to the obedience of Christ;"* God knew that the mind is what Satan would try to control and destroy. This is why God commands in Philippians 2:5, *"Let this mind be in you, which was also in Christ Jesus:"* God continues to warn the Christian about protecting their mind when He commands in Ephesians 4:23, *"And be renewed in the spirit of your mind;"* Your mind is so important because it controls your spirit, and it controls how you look at the Scriptures.

The mind in the Scriptures is defined as the heart. One reason we are warned about guarding our heart or mind is because whatever we allow to influence our mind eventually dictates who we become. Proverbs 4:23 shows us this when it says, *"Keep thy heart with all diligence; for out of it are the issues of life."* If Satan can get control of your mind by constantly feeding your mind with the wrong information, he can eventually change what you believe and how you live. Don't make the mistake of thinking that Satan is not trying to control your mind; he is! You are going to have to keep your mind under control because it is the battleground where every spiritual battle is fought.

2. Use the Philippians 4:8 model as the controlling rule to dictate which information you receive.

Philippians 4:8 says, *"Finally, brethren, whatsoever things are true, whatsoever things are honest, whatsoever things are just, whatsoever things are pure, whatsoever things are lovely, whatsoever things are of good report; if there be any virtue, and if there be any praise, think on these things."* This, my friend, is the rule by which the Christian should measure all information they receive. If the information you receive does not fall into one of these categories, you should be sure that you block any information that comes from that source.

When using the Philippians 4:8 model, all you have to do is ask yourself if what you are watching in the news media or looking at on social media is what this verse prescribes. For instance, is what you see true, honest, and so forth? It really comes down to one phrase in this verse, *"...whatsoever things are of good report..."* This one phrase will cause you not to follow most of what is being propagated through these medias. It doesn't matter if it is true or honest, is it a good report?

The danger with social media and the 24-hour news media is that most of the information they feed doesn't fall under the Philippians 4:8 guide. You may think that if you use this verse as the rule in determining the sources of your information that you will be out-of-touch, but it is better to be out-of-touch than to be fed the negative and false information that will pollute your mind and spirit. Your mind only thinks on the information you receive, and that is why you must use Philippians 4:8 as the rule as to whether or not you should allow that source into your life.

3. You should choose from whom you get information.

The danger with constantly overloading yourself with information from the news and social media is that you are not in control of what you are feeding your mind. Romans 6:16 commands, *"Know ye not, that to whom ye yield yourselves servants to obey, his servants ye are to whom ye obey; whether of sin unto death, or of obedience unto righteousness?"* Your mind can't help but think on the things which you feed it. If you allow your mind to be overloaded with the news and social media, you will become whatever information you read and watch. If you want to live a life of peace, you are going to have to be spiritually minded, which only happens by avoiding the information overload that comes from these sources. God warns us in Romans 8:6, *"For to be carnally minded is death; but to be spiritually minded is life and peace."* You need to be in control of the incoming information instead of allowing sources of carnality to feed your mind and control you.

4. Don't make media the background noise.

One mistake many people make is that they allow the 24-hour news media to be background noise. My friend, this will affect your spirit. Background noise often causes you to miss the moving of God in your life. It was the *"still small voice"* in Elijah's life that brought him out of his discouragement. It was in the quiet of night that Samuel heard God's calling in his life. There is no way you are going to hear the voice of God in your life when you have the constant background noise of worldly information coming at you through the news and social medias.

5. You are not obligated to follow anyone.

Social media has a way of causing many to follow people who they normally would have nothing to do with because of their lifestyles. However, when we are asked in social media to "friend" someone or invited to "follow" them, many are afraid they will offend them if they don't accept their invitation. Let me make this clear, there is only one person you are obligated to follow, and that is Jesus Christ. Jesus says in John 12:26, *"If any man serve me, let him follow me; and where I am, there shall also my servant be: if any man serve me, him will my Father honour."* There is certainly nothing wrong with "friending" or "following" individuals, but remember that you are choosing to let them influence you with their information.

Let me also give a friendly warning that when someone begins to publish information you shouldn't see or hear, cut off your communication with them. Colossians 3:8 commands, *"But now ye also put off all these; anger, wrath, malice, blasphemy, filthy communication out of your mouth."* Psalm 101:3 also says, *"I will set no wicked thing before mine eyes: I hate the work of them that turn aside; it shall not cleave to me."* Whenever you see anything or hear anything that the LORD would not be pleased with, immediately cut that source away from your life so that your mind and spirit can stay free from the filth of the world.

6. Validate before embracing as truth.

Just because the news media says something doesn't make it true. Likewise, just because you see something on social media doesn't make it a fact. Many have put themselves in a bad situation by repeating something they heard on the news as fact, or believing the lies they read on social media before they ever learned if that information was true. God says in Proverbs 18:13, *"He that answereth a matter before he heareth it, it is folly and shame unto him."* There have been many times that a ministry or person has been slandered because of the lies propagated through social media. Just because someone you know says something is true on social media doesn't mean that it is true. God says in Proverbs 25:2, *"It is the glory of God to conceal a thing: but the honour of kings is to search out a matter."* Before you embrace something as truth, you would be wise to search it out before spreading something that will hurt someone's character or reputation.

Moreover, you can never take back all the damage once something has been said or posted on social media. Churches are constantly dealing with the onslaught of lies propagated by the Devil's social and news media. Sadly, many Christians have helped the Devil through their own posts by sharing or commenting on things they **assume** to be true. Even if what is being said is true, it doesn't need to be spread so the world can use it as a tool to portray all churches, preachers or Christians in such light. You would do better to pray and commit the situation to God than to spread that which could be harmful to the cause of Christ.

7. Schedule your information time.

If you are going to keep from information overload, you are going to have to learn to control the amount of time you spend getting it. Romans 6:16 warns, *"Know ye not, that to whom ye yield yourselves servants to obey, his servants ye are to whom ye obey; whether of sin unto death, or of obedience unto righteousness?"* You don't have to be a servant to media; rather, you should be the ruler who controls how much time you spend getting information from news or social media. It would be wise to schedule the amount of time that you choose to look at social media, and don't make it an all-day constant browsing and feeding frenzy of information to overload your mind with information you don't need.

8. Will the information you're getting glorify the LORD?

1 Corinthians 10:31 commands, *"Whether therefore ye eat, or drink, or whatsoever ye do, do all to the glory of God."* You should constantly ask yourself if the content of the

people you follow or friend on social media glorifies the LORD? If the content someone posts doesn't glorify the LORD, you should stop following them. They have no right to intrude into your life with the filthy pictures or gossip they posts on their social media platforms.

Furthermore, most news is not going to bring glory to God. I know that we live in this world, and we should know what is happening in our world, but you don't have to let the news dictate your whole day. Most news media rehashes the same news all day. You can only get so much about the same news without eventually it overloading your mind and spirit. Moreover, if a certain news source is constantly showing things that are not Christ-honoring, you should consider getting your news from a different source.

9. Yield to the Holy Spirit.

Galatians 5:16 says, *"This I say then, Walk in the Spirit, and ye shall not fulfil the lust of the flesh."* If you are going to "walk in the Spirit," you are going to have to yield to Him. The best way to control the influx of information is by continually yielding yourself to the Holy Spirit. Let the Holy Spirit control your mind, and not the news and social media. If you yield to the Holy Spirit, you can keep the information which feeds your mind wholesome, and the wholesome information will result in living a godly life. Be careful about allowing the ease of information to become a source that overloads your mind with information that quenches the Holy Spirit in your life. If you yield to the Spirit instead of yielding to the news and social media, you will find yourself walking in the Spirit and being a Christian who lives a joyful life.

Chapter 5

THE REDEFINITION OF MARRIAGE

Marriage has been under attack since it was instituted in the Garden of Eden. It is interesting that Satan didn't attack Adam before Eve was created, but he chose to focus his attack against the both of them through a personal attack against their marriage. Satan knew that he could destroy more people through a broken marriage than he could by personally attacking an individual.

Satan's ploy of destruction has not changed today. He is still trying to destroy lives by attacking marriages, and especially by trying to redefine the definition of marriage. He knows that the youth will miss out on the influences they need if he can destroy the institution of marriage. What many don't take into consideration is that children are safest inside the confines of a stable and spiritual marriage. If Satan destroys a marriage, he not only destroys the couple and what they were doing for the LORD, but he also destroys the influence those children will have for many generations.

Look at the destruction that Satan caused by breaking down the first marriage. Because Adam and Eve's marriage suffered through sin, their children learned all the bad qualities that destroy a life. Cain would have never killed Abel had Adam and Eve's marriage stayed the way that God intended for a marriage to be. The influences of the sin on their marriage is still felt today in every individual's life because the sin nature is passed down from generation to generation. Romans 5:12 shows us this when it says, *"Wherefore, as by one man sin entered into the world, and death by sin; and so death passed upon all men, for that all have sinned:"* If Satan can destroy marriages, he knows that he can change the soul of a nation.

Throughout the years, Satan's attack has attempted to redefine what God intended for a marriage to be. When you redefine marriage, you change its purpose and the influences it can have on children, church and society. There are five ways that Satan tries to redefine marriage.

1. Satan tries to redefine the Scriptural roles of the husband and wife.

We have already talked about the roles of marriage in this book, but let me remind you what those roles are so you can see how Satan is trying to redefine them. The role of the husband is to love his wife and to be the leader of the home. Ephesians 5:25 says, *"Husbands, love your wives, even as Christ also loved the church, and gave himself for it;"* You will notice it doesn't say humor her by making her think you are listening and caring for her, but you are to love her in the same manner that Christ loved the church. Furthermore, the husband is to be the head of the home. Ephesians 5:23 says, *"For the husband is the head of the wife..."* It doesn't matter that this is politically incorrect, God intended for the husband to be the leader of the home.

God also clearly defines the role of the wife when He says in Colossians 3:18, *"Wives, submit yourselves unto your own husbands, as it is fit in the Lord."* When a wife submits to her husband's leadership, you will find the marriage will be strengthened because the roles for both husband and wife are clearly defined.

Satan has tried to redefine these roles by influencing society to belittle the male leadership in the home. The equal rights movement is not about trying to get men to treat ladies properly, but it is an attempt to shame men into not leading. If Satan can redefine the roles of marriage, he is well on his way to destroying that marriage and family.

2. Satan is trying to redefine marriage through the "Marriage Equality" definition.

Who would have ever thought that we would have to define that marriage is between a man and a woman? We live in times when the push is to accept same-sex unions as marriage. Let me make this clear; it is not same-sex marriage, it is same-sex sin. God never intended for men or women to marry the same gender.

When God instituted the first marriage, he gave the pattern and definition that marriage is between a man and a woman. Genesis 2:24 says, *"Therefore shall a man leave his father and his mother, and shall cleave unto his wife: and they shall be one flesh."* God further defined marriage in Genesis 1:28 by telling Adam and Eve, *"And God blessed them, and God said unto them, Be fruitful, and multiply, and replenish the earth…"* Notice that they were to *"multiply, and replenish."* Only a man and woman can recreate. It is impossible for sodomites to reproduce. They don't reproduce, but they recruit. Satan has tried to redefine the definition of marriage for the sake of destroying its purpose which is life. One of the greatest arguments against same-sex "marriage" not being scriptural is that they cannot *"multiply, and replenish."*

3. Satan is trying to redefine marriage through divorce.

God's original purpose for marriage was not only for one man and one woman, but it was for them to stay married until death. Matthew 19:5-6 says, *"...For this cause shall a man leave father and mother, and shall cleave to his wife: and they twain shall be one flesh? Wherefore they are no more twain, but one flesh. What therefore God hath joined together, let not man put asunder."* God never intended for a couple to get divorced. In fact, the only reason divorce became an option was because of the hardness of man's heart.

Satan has successfully started the redefinition of marriage by getting people to accept that divorce is normal. According to polls, the majority of Americans believe that divorce is morally acceptable. When you break down the wall of staying married until death, you will then find the definitions of marriage in other areas will begin to fall.

4. Satan is trying to redefine marriage by breaking down the walls of mystique.

We live in times when many pastors believe it is okay to open the doors of the bedroom for all to see. Let me make this very clear; your marriage is on dangerous grounds when you begin to talk to others about what goes on in the bedroom. Hebrews 13:4 says, *"Marriage is honourable in all, and the bed undefiled..."* There should be a mystique about a couple. Nobody should know what goes on in private between a husband and wife. Several times throughout the Scriptures God talks about a husband and wife being *"one flesh."* What they do should in private should never be talked about in public.

Satan has fooled many people into believing that we need to talk about the privacy of marriage in public settings with couples, but he also knows when this is done that the walls of mystique are broken down. It is amazing throughout the Scriptures that God keeps the bed a private matter; He never goes into detail because a husband and wife can figure things out without having to expose their own marriage. If Satan can redefine the boundaries as to what is acceptable to talk about concerning the mystique of marriage, he can open a couple up to many temptations that many marriages cannot overcome.

5. Satan is trying to redefine marriage by changing the purpose of marriage.

As mentioned previously, a couple is to *"multiply, and replenish."* If Satan can get a couple focused more on their careers than on having and rearing children, he can destroy that home and society. It is sad to see many choosing not to have children because it keeps them from having a "successful" career. Everyone knows that somebody has to stay home and rear the children once they have them. Because of the love of money, couples will sacrifice children for the sake of making money. Satan has destroyed many marriages by getting both husband and wife to focus on their careers. This has resulted in a wedge being driven between them because they are never together, and it causes great disharmony in the marriage. It has also kept them from obeying God's command to have children and rearing children in godly homes, which is the future of carrying on to the next generation what the Scriptures teach.

Why is it so important for Satan to try to redefine the definitions of marriage? I believe there are four reasons why Satan is so intent on redefining marriage.

1. It is God's institution.

Satan is against anything that God is for. His goal is to destroy anything God starts because it hurts His cause. God created life, so Satan tries to destroy life because he hates God. God instituted the church, so Satan tries to destroy the church because he hates that the church carries the Gospel of Jesus Christ. Satan tries to destroy your marriage and the definition of marriage because he wants to destroy what God has started. The whole redefinition of marriage is about destroying what God instituted.

2. Redefining marriage takes God's Word out of the marriage.

One reason Satan is so adamant about redefining marriage is because its definition comes straight from the Scriptures. Satan hates the Word of God and will do anything in his power to change it. If Satan can change the definition of marriage, he can prove that God's Word is no longer relevant for every person today. From the first temptation, Satan has attempted to redefine God's Word so that he can destroy what God originally set up for man to follow.

3. Marriage is a picture of Christ and the church.

Marriage is a picture of Christ and His future bride, the church. Isn't it interesting that in Ephesians 5:25-27, God shows how marriage is a picture of Christ and the church. One of the reasons society hates the church so much is because it pictures the relationship Christ has with the believer, and it also pictures that salvation only comes through Christ; thus, you have society trying to destroy the marriage institution. If Satan can redefine marriage, he will succeed at redefining salvation and the church.

4. A scriptural marriage produces strong churches.

Don't fool yourself into believing that a strong marriage has no positive or negative impact on the church. It does! Every strong church is filled with strong marriages. If Satan can destroy the marriage through redefining it, he succeeds in destroying the church and the impact it can have on reaching the lost for Jesus Christ.

With these thoughts in mind, let me give you several statements to help you keep your marriage strong and within God's definition of a true marriage.

1. God originated marriage between a man and a woman.

I don't want to belabor this definition, but we must never forget God's original intent for marriage was between a man and a woman. Anything other than a man and a woman in a marriage is an abomination to God. Romans 1:28 makes it clear about God's mindset of those who try to redefine marriage when He says, *"And even as they did not like to retain God in their knowledge, God gave them over to a reprobate mind..."*

2. God's original intent for marriage was no divorce.

Remember what Matthew 19:6 says, *"...What therefore God hath joined together, let not man put asunder."* Divorce must never be an option in a marriage if that marriage is going to stay strong. My advice from the Scriptures is that working out your problems is God's way of solving marital issues rather than divorce. When divorce is no longer an option, finding a way to work out your problems will become a tool to make your marriage strong.

3. Strong marriages are grounded in God's Word.

You cannot have a strong marriage without the manual that describes the definition of marriage, which is the Word of God. Psalm 127:1 says, *"Except the LORD build the house, they labour in vain that build it..."* The LORD cannot build your marriage if you are not spending time in the Scriptures. The foundation of your marriage must be the Word of God if you want it to stay strong and weather the storms that life brings against it.

4. Strong marriages are transparent.

The greatest destroyer of marriage is deception. At the core of every marriage problem is lies and deception. If you remove the lies and the deception, you remove what destroys a marriage. John 8:32 says, *"And ye shall know the truth, and the truth shall make you free."* One of the themes in my marriage and home has been, no secrets. When you remove the secrets in a marriage and live by transparency, you remove the tools Satan uses to destroy it. My friend, nobody wins when secrets are being kept between a couple. God says that a married couple is *"one flesh;"* therefore, as one flesh knows what the whole body is doing, so ought the husband and wife know about each other. Don't let deception and deceit infiltrate into your marriage if you want it to stay strong.

5. Strong marriages establish rules, boundaries and limitations.

Anything that is going to stay strong must have rules, boundaries and limitations. There is nothing wrong with establishing rules by which each spouse lives. If you don't have rules, boundaries and limitations, you are sure to do something that will destroy your marriage. Don't fight against the established rules in your marriage; they are there to protect you from the outside sources that desire to destroy your marriage.

6. The answer to fighting societal attack against the marriage is to keep your marriage strong.

The best way to fight against society's attempt to redefine marriage is to make your marriage strong. If you make your marriage strong, your children will see it and desire what you have. I think the only thing that has given credence to Satan's redefinition campaign against the marriage is that many children grow up in dysfunctional homes because of broken marriages, and they want nothing to do with marriage because of what they had to endure as children. Let me encourage you to make your marriage strong. If your marriage is struggling, get help from someone who can help you identify the areas that are destroying your marriage. Redefining marriage will become a thing of the past when children grow up seeing an example of what God originally intended for marriage to be.

I truly believe that other than your relationship with Christ, the greatest relationship is found between a husband and wife. If you work hard at making your marriage what it ought to be, the next generation will look at it and desire that same relationship with a spouse as God defines it, and Satan will lose his campaign to redefine marriage.

Chapter 6

THE SOCIAL ACCEPTANCE PRESSURE

Social acceptance is an every generation battle that always leads to regretful decisions. Teenagers are often the ones who are accused of falling for the pressures of social acceptance, but adults are just as guilty. The pressure of social acceptance is not an age-associated problem; it is a problem that deals with our selfish desire to be liked by the in-crowd.

We often see social acceptance pressures revealed through clothing and hairstyle fads. Every generation can look back with regret at some of the ridiculous styles they have fallen for or have seen in their lifetime. It never fails to bring a blush to the face when shown a picture of ourselves wearing the faddish clothing of a by-gone era.

Likewise, some of the things we were willing to do to be socially accepted have brought regret to many adults. This is one reason so many adults admonish youth not to surrender to the pressure of social acceptance from their peers. Many adults realize that the fallacy of yielding to their peers caused them to do things they wish they had never done; but for the sake of being accepted by their peers, they were willing to do things they normally would not do.

Sadly, the pressures of social acceptance don't stop at the door of youth, clothing or current fads. The pressure of social acceptance is also a part of Christianity. I am amazed at how many people look for the next big church or movement to jump into without one time looking at where it leads or what it does to your beliefs. In my lifetime, I have watched many Christians who once stood for something turn against it because it was not socially accepted by the current "big" church. These people who once used to stand for truth are no longer standing where they stood because they believe what they are doing is right, but they are standing where they stand simply because it is the socially accepted stance of the in-crowd.

Many fads have worked their way through the independent, fundamental Baptist movement in my lifetime. I remember when the bus ministry was the big thing; every church started a bus ministry because it was socially acceptable. Not long afterward, the Christian school movement became a fad, so many churches started a Christian school because it was what everyone was doing. The next thing was to see as many people saved regardless of the biblical responsibility to follow up on their converts. That soon passed with everyone focusing on getting as many people baptized as they could. The next thing was that every church started discipleship programs thinking that was the answer to building large churches. I have watched churches start addiction ministries, colleges, remodel their auditoriums to look like the bigger churches, and so many more fads that have swept through our movement. Each of these things by themselves are not bad, but many only did them because it was the socially accepted thing to do at the time in the fundamental Baptist movement. What many never realized is that you don't do these things because they are a fad or because they build a large church, you do these things because they are right and because they build people. My point is that even our churches have fallen for the social fads that will soon be dropped for the next "great idea." It is not that these things are bad, but the pressure of social acceptance is seen in every part of life.

Part of the reason we are so prone to the pressure of social acceptance is because we want to be liked by everyone. This pressure is found in the Scriptures by many who did things they normally would not have done. For the sake of being socially accepted, they did something only to regret it.

For instance, Israel wanted a king, not because it was right, but because they wanted to be *"like all the nations."* (1 Samuel 8:5) In Exodus 32, Aaron made a golden calf for Israel to worship because of the pressure they put on him to make them gods to worship. Saul made the mistake of succumbing to the pressure of social acceptance when he foolishly intruded on a sacrifice that was only intended for the priest to administer. His reasoning was that he saw the people were *"scattered"* from him, and he didn't want to lose their approval. This act, in 1 Samuel 13, led to him not following the LORD's command to completely destroy the Amalekites because the pressure of the people was to save the best for themselves.

The pressure of social acceptance is also found in the New Testament when Peter denied the church, his faith, and his God because of the pressure of the crowd with whom he associated. Maybe, the most notable person who fell for the pressure of social acceptance was Pilate. Mark 15:15 says, *"And so Pilate, willing to content the people, released Barabbas unto them, and delivered Jesus, when he had scourged him, to be crucified."* Pilate knew that Jesus was not worthy of death, but for the sake of being socially accepted, he yielded to their pressure and allowed Jesus to be unjustly crucified.

The pressure of social acceptance brings several dangers with it. Those who yield to this pressure from the world and spiritual realm often find themselves on the wrong side of truth. There are five dangers in yielding to the pressure of social acceptance.

1. Truth no longer becomes your focal point.

When you allow the pressure of society to become the influence of what you will and will not do, you will soon find yourself on the opposite side of truth. Psalm 119:105 says, *"Thy word is a lamp unto my feet, and a light unto my path."* The Word of God is to be the focal point to determine what you do in life. You can't obey God and be socially accepted at the same time. James 4:4 reminds us of this when it says, *"…whosoever therefore will be a friend of the world is the enemy of God."* You are either going to be rejected by the world and right with God, or disobedient to God and socially accepted by the world. As Luke 16:13 reminds us, *"No servant can serve two masters: for either he will hate the one, and love the other; or else he will hold to the one, and despise the other. Ye cannot serve God and mammon."*

2. The next crowd becomes your crowd.

One of the mistakes of looking to be socially accepted is that you always follow the next big crowd, whether or not they are doing right. I'm amazed at how people who once used to have Christ-honoring standards lower their standards to be socially accepted by their peers. The reason they have lowered their standards is because the next crowd doesn't have the same Christ-honoring standards as the previous crowd. If you always look to be accepted by the next big crowd, you will one day find yourself doing things you once said you would never do. Let me remind you of Leviticus 20:7 which says, *"Sanctify yourselves therefore, and be ye holy: for I am the LORD your God."* Stop looking to the crowd for social acceptance, and look to God for His approval.

3. The crowd is rarely right.

Hebrews 13:13 says, *"Let us go forth therefore unto him without the camp, bearing his reproach."* You will never find the approval of Jesus Christ if you are looking to the crowd for social acceptance. As Hebrews 13:13 reminds us, you will be a *"reproach"* to the world when you follow Christ. All you have to do is look back at history to see how often the crowd was right, and you will soon find that you are better to be a *"reproach"* to the world so you can be right with Christ.

4. Yielding to social acceptance is idolatry.

Matthew 6:33 commands, *"But seek ye first the kingdom of God, and his righteousness; and all these things shall be added unto you."* An idol is anything which usurps the place of God in your heart or life. 1 John 5:21 commands the Christian, *"Little children, keep yourselves from idols…"* When you yield to the social acceptance pressure, you are putting something before God. The only one who you should yield to is God; anything else is idolatry.

5. When will you stop moving?

The problem with trying to be socially accepted is that you will always move positionally to be accepted by whatever crowd you are in. The question that then must be asked is, when will you stop moving? The problem with always yielding to whatever is socially acceptable by the current movement in Christianity is that the movement is never the basis for truth. The reason you must base whatever you do on the Scriptures is because truth is the only thing that never changes. The fact that you are willing to move proves that you are moving to be socially accepted.

How do we deal with the pressure of social acceptance?

1. Look at every decision through the prism of God's Word.

If you are going to overcome the pressure of social acceptance, you are going to have to stop trying to make the Word of God fit your lifestyle, and instead transform your lifestyle to the Word of God. Romans 12:2 says, *"And be not conformed to this world: but be ye transformed by the renewing of your mind, that ye may prove what is that good, and acceptable, and perfect, will of God."* The Christian is never to conform to the world; rather, they are to transform their mind to fit the will of God, and His will is only found in the Scriptures. When you start letting God's Word define your actions, thoughts, styles and beliefs, you will find that the pressure you put on yourself to be socially accepted will no longer be an influence in your thinking.

2. Yield to the Holy Spirit instead of the spirit of social acceptance.

Ephesians 5:18 says, *"And be not drunk with wine, wherein is excess; but be filled with the Spirit;"* When you are filled with the Spirit, you will find that the things of the world will no longer be appetizing. The biggest reason so many people fail to overcome the pressure of social acceptance is because they are living to fulfill the lusts of the flesh instead of yielding to the Holy Spirit.

3. Remember that there is a tomorrow to today's decision.

Galatians 6:7 says, *"Be not deceived; God is not mocked: for whatsoever a man soweth, that shall he also reap."* You cannot sow to the flesh without reaping its consequences. You must always remember that what you do today will always have ramifications you must live with tomorrow. You must ask yourself if you want to live with tomorrow's consequences the next time you are tempted to yield to the pressures of being socially accepted. You may enjoy the pleasures that social acceptance brings today, but tomorrow's consequence is often greater than one ever thought it would be.

4. Remember the next generation.

One of the biggest reasons you should never yield to the pressure of social acceptance is because you are teaching the next generation how to live. Abram never thought that going to Egypt would influence Lot the way it did, but Lot suffered greatly because he was exposed to the world because Abram yielded to the pressure of social acceptance.

You must always remember that the next generation will always take what you do today to the next step. If you stand in truth, you will never have to worry about the next generation being exposed to things which they should never see or do. Always keep in mind that someone is following you, and if you are constantly changing to conform to be socially accepted, they will also continue that trend to their own detriment.

5. Be an influence instead of being influenced.

Ephesians 5:11 says, *"And have no fellowship with the unfruitful works of darkness, but rather reprove them."* God wants the Christian to be the one influencing instead of them being influenced. That is why he says in Romans 12:2, *"And be not conformed to this world: but be ye transformed by the renewing of your mind, that ye may prove what is that good, and acceptable, and perfect, will of God."*

You will never change the world when the world is constantly changing you. God says in Matthew 5:14, *"Ye are the light of the world…"* Light always influences darkness. You never see a light overcome by darkness, but darkness is always overcome by light. That is why God continued in Matthew 5:16 by commanding, *"Let your light so shine before men, that they may see your good works, and glorify your Father which is in heaven."* Christian, you are to be the one who influences the world. When you yield to the pressure of social acceptance, you are not letting your light shine. Your light only shines brightly for Christ and influences the world when you stop yielding to the pressure of social acceptance.

6. Walk with those who are Christ-focused.

Proverbs 13:20 says, *"He that walketh with wise men shall be wise: but a companion of fools shall be destroyed."* You are influenced by those with whom you spend time. The best way to overcome the pressure of social acceptance is to spend time with those who are Christ-focused. People who are Christ-focused are not interested in what others around them think; they are only interested in pleasing the LORD. When you spend time with Christ-focused people, the pressure will be to stay focused on Christ and His Word.

The pressure of social acceptance is a great pressure that every generation must fight. If Satan can get you focused on what the crowd around you thinks, he can eventually get culture to define you instead of the Scriptures. Satan doesn't care if you yield to the positive pressures of being socially accepted because he knows you will change if you will yield to anything other than God. Satan uses culture to pressure you into change. You must determine to stay focused on the Scriptures, and only let God's Word define who you are and what you do. It is only when the Scriptures are your focal point of actions and beliefs that you will always find yourself doing the will of God and overcoming the pressures of social acceptance.

CHAPTER 7

REDEFINING MORALITY

There used to be a day in my lifetime when society held to public morals. There were things you would never talk about in public because it was morally unacceptable. As a boy, my siblings and I were never allowed to talk about what happened in the bedroom or even make innuendoes about a person's biological characteristics. If we even used the three letter word about being intimate with someone, our mouth was washed out with soap. Our home was not an anomaly in holding these high moral standards for it was commonplace in most households.

Somehow we have lost our blush when it comes to morality. Our society has lost its shock and embarrassment when hearing or seeing immorality in public. What used to shock us as something immoral has now become billboard advertising along the highways. Topics that used to bring a blush of embarrassment to the face when discussed are now common conversation and programming on nightly television shows. The innuendos and jokes that leave the mind wandering into places it has no business wandering are commonplace, acceptable, and some even think they are humorous. What once used to be considered vulgar and unacceptable is now a common part of daily conversations.

Even our pulpits seem to have lost their conscience on morality. There used to be a day when you didn't have to worry about what the preacher was going to say about marriage from the pulpit. Now, preachers excuse off-color conversations about what happens in the bedroom as a need to help keep marriages happy. My friend, some things should never be discussed in public. There are some things that a married couple should only discuss between themselves. There are some things that should never be discussed in a public forum.

Today, books are written by Christian authors to supposedly help couples in their marriage but they are nothing more than pornography put into words. Let me be clear about this; if something can't be sold to youth because it would open doors that they should never open until they are married, then we shouldn't condone the immorality that is propagated in these books even if they come from a Christian viewpoint. It is sad when churches have done just as much to pollute the minds of our youth through "Christian" books as Hollywood does through their filthy programming.

The goal of redefining morality has been an ongoing attack to continually push godly morals out of society. Let me point out that immorality is not just a modern-day battle, but it can be found all the way back when Israel took their clothes off to dance around a golden calf. Satan has tried to redefine the morality of every society and age because morality is always associated with God and holiness. If Satan can get society to change its standard of morality and what is accepted as moral, he can get us to reject God as our accepted standard of morality.

The changing of morals in society can easily be seen in Hollywood. In the early 1950's, couples were required to sleep in separate beds to uphold the moral codes of society. The popular *I Love Lucy* show was one of the first programs to navigate into a couple sleeping in the same bed, and it wasn't the main characters of the programming who did it. The boundary they crossed in that show doesn't even cross our minds as immoral today. Why? Because society has successfully redefined the boundaries of morality to the point that anyone who holds to scriptural morality is considered weird and out-of-touch with society. My friend, it is better to be out-of-touch with society than to lose your morals and purity.

God commands the Christian in Leviticus 20:7, *"Sanctify yourselves therefore, and be ye holy: for I am the LORD your God."* God reinforces the importance of Christians being holy in 1 Peter 1:15 when He says, *"But as he which hath called you is holy, so be ye holy in all manner of conversation;"* You will notice that God's standard for the Christian is holiness. Satan knows that the Christian will no longer be able to make a difference if he can get them to redefine their scriptural morals.

God wants His children to be different. God told Israel in Exodus 11:7, *"But against any of the children of Israel shall not a dog move his tongue, against man or beast: that ye may know how that the LORD doth put a difference between the Egyptians and Israel."* If God commanded Israel to be different, why would He expect any less from those whom He has redeemed from sin? The reason God wants us to be different is so that we can make a difference in this world. You will never influence the world if you are like them. What enables you to make a difference is that you are different. Keeping scriptural morals is important to making a difference in this world and in the lives of those whom we are trying to help. Let me show you several reasons as to why we should keep scriptural and holy morals.

1. So we can serve the LORD without restraint.

A moral life gives confidence and boldness. God says in 2 Peter 3:14, *"Wherefore, beloved, seeing that ye look for such things, be diligent that ye may be found of him in peace, without spot, and blameless."* A life *"without spot"* is a life that lives according to scriptural morals. Living a moral life allows you to live a blameless life. A blameless life gives you the confidence and boldness you need to point others to Christ. It is imperative to keep your morals high so that you don't have to live life looking over your shoulder worrying what someone may say about you. Though society may change its morals, Christians need to hold to the holy morals of the Scriptures.

2. So our relationship with our spouse is not damaged.

In Ephesians 5, God gives specific advice to married couples on how to keep their marriage strong. One of the admonitions God gives is found in verses 27-28 which says, *"That he might present it to himself a glorious church, not having spot, or wrinkle, or any such thing; but that it should be holy and without blemish. So ought men to love their wives as their own bodies. He that loveth his wife loveth himself."* How are men to love their wife? They are to love them by living their life without *"having spot, or wrinkle."* In other words, God is showing that a moral life will keep your marriage strong. One of the main reasons you need to be sure to live according to the morals of the Scriptures is so that the Devil can't use immorality to destroy the trust between the husband and wife.

3. So our youth can walk down the aisle as virgins on their wedding day.

For many years, it has been preached that young people are to stay pure so they can give themselves as a virgin for their spouse. Let me again declare that it is still right for young people to be a virgin on their wedding day. One of the reasons you need to keep your morals high is so that your children will not be tempted with immorality. God kept the standard of morality so high that He commands the opposite gender not to touch. 1 Corinthians 7:1 says, *"Now concerning the things whereof ye wrote unto me: It is good for a man not to touch a woman."* God knows that if a young person never touches the opposite gender, they will never lose their virginity. You need to keep scriptural morals if you don't want your children to have to fight the temptations that the flesh can throw at them.

4. So our minds are filled with holiness and not immorality.

One of the biggest battlefields in the Christian life, if not the biggest, is in our minds. This is why God commands the Christian in 1 Peter 1:13, *"Wherefore gird up the loins of your mind..."* God knows that most of the battles that the Christian will fight is in the mind. That is why He commands in 2 Corinthians 10:5, *"Casting down imaginations, and every high thing that exalteth itself against the knowledge of God, and bringing into captivity every thought to the obedience of Christ;"* You are going to have to live by scriptural morals if you are going to keep your mind from wicked imaginations. Every wicked imagination that you fight is because at some point you accepted society's morals instead of keeping the morals of the Scriptures. If you want to keep your mind thinking in a holy manner, you are going to have to allow the scriptural morals to be your protection from immorality.

5. So our homes and churches are safe havens to rear godly children.

The only way we are going to rear godly children in the nurture and admonition of the LORD is by keeping the morals of the Scriptures in our homes and churches. The morals of the home and the church should not be different. Children should be able to grow up in a place where their minds are insulated from the immorality of the world. Your children will never live like they are supposed to live according to the Scriptures if the home and church don't keep scriptural morals. Psalm 132:12 says, *"If thy children will keep my covenant and my testimony that I shall teach them, their children shall also sit upon thy throne for evermore."* The hope of the next generation continuing to live according to the Scriptures is for this generation to have morals patterned after the Scriptures. Children should never be exposed to the world in the church or at home. The morals you have are the walls you build to keep your children from having their minds polluted by the world. We should not isolate our children from the world because they have to live in it, but they should be insulated from the world by living in an atmosphere with scriptural morals.

6. So that our lives are distinctly different from the world.

Romans 12:2 says, *"And be not conformed to this world: but be ye transformed by the renewing of your mind, that ye may prove what is that good, and acceptable, and perfect, will of God."* The Christian is often the only picture of Christ that the world will ever see. If the Christian has accepted the morals of modern society, the world will never get a clear picture of Christ. Christian, the purpose of transforming your life from worldly immorality to scriptural morality is so that your life will prove to the world that God's way of living is the best life to live.

Because it is important not to accept the redefined morals of society, we must ask ourselves how we are to hold onto the morals of the Scriptures. Let me give you seven ways how to hold strongly to scriptural morals.

1. Let the Word of God be the measurement of morality.

Several years ago a pastor disagreed with me on my standard of morality because he said that the present culture and one's conscience should dictate our standard of morality. The problem with allowing one's conscience or culture to dictate morality is that both will change with time. 1 John 2:7 shows that these things change when it says, *"And the world passeth away, and the lust thereof..."* There is only one standard that never changes, and that is God's Word. Psalm 119:89 makes this clear when it says, *"For ever, O LORD, thy word is settled in heaven."* Morality is not a relative measure because it is an absolute; therefore, only God's Word can be the measurement of morality because it never changes.

2. Always be proper with the opposite gender.

If we are going to keep scriptural morals, we are going to have to live morally with each other. I have said for years that those who change their morals are people who want to validate their immoral heart. You should live in such a manner that nobody could ever morally question your actions with the opposite gender.

3. Never allow yourself to be alone with the opposite gender other than your immediate family.

I know for some, this seems to be ridiculous, but if you are never alone with the opposite gender, you won't ever be immoral with them. Common sense alone should caution you never to allow yourself to be in a situation where your morals could be questioned. Even if the questions of others are not true, you have no recourse of defense if you allow yourself to be alone with the opposite gender. The best way to keep yourself morally right is never to allow yourself to be alone with someone of the opposite gender.

4. Keep your conversations pure.

One's conversation often tells much about their heart. If your conversations are held to the standard of purity, you will never have to leave the morals of the Scriptures to defend your actions. Ephesians 4:29 says, *"Let no corrupt communication proceed out of your mouth, but that which is good to the use of edifying, that it may minister grace unto the hearers."* If the words you say are impure words, they will corrupt how you live. What you say does influence how you act.

5. Ask the Holy Spirit to keep you from those moments that would try to break down the walls of morality.

One of the greatest prayers you can pray on a daily basis is for the LORD to deliver you from those moments that would change your morals. One of the things that Jesus taught in the LORD's prayer was to ask, *"And lead us not into temptation, but deliver us from evil…"* (Matthew 6:13) Only the Holy Spirit of God can keep you from those times when temptation would damage your morals and testimony. My friend, your morals are the shield which protects your testimony. If the Holy Spirit can keep you from the time when you would choose to compromise your morals, He can also keep you from damaging your testimony for Jesus Christ.

6. Associate with the right people.

Wrong associations have ruined many morals. Whenever I see someone lowering their morals and going down the wrong path, I always know that they are associated with someone who is influencing them. Paul asked in Galatians 5:7, *"Ye did run well; who did hinder you that ye should not obey the truth?"* A "who" always affects the "what" that you do. If you want to keep yourself morally right, you need to keep associations with those who live a moral life. Many people have associated with someone of lower morals in an attempt to influence them, only to find that their morals were affected. Keeping the right associations is imperative to keeping scriptural morals.

7. Be accountable to someone.

The mistake the people made in the Book of Judges was that they were only accountable to themselves. Proverbs 29:15 says, *"The rod and reproof give wisdom: but a child left to himself bringeth his mother to shame."* If a child who has no accountability brings shame to their mother, so an adult who has no accountability will bring shame to their Saviour. Being accountable to someone helps you to keep your morals intact.

Christian, Satan would love for you to redefine your morals. He will do everything in his power to accomplish this because when you change your morals, you will no longer hold to the fact that the King James Bible is inerrant. Satan's attack to redefine morals is an attack against the Word of God. Don't fall for the redefinition of morals. If something was right or wrong in the past, it is still right and wrong today. If you always hold true to the morals of the Scriptures, you will never regret the joy that their protection brings.

CHAPTER 8

JUDICIAL INJUSTICE

It's not fair! Every child has said those words when they saw an injustice or felt that they were treated unjustly. They saw someone get away with something and they knew that if they had done the same thing they would have gotten into trouble. Whether or not we like it, life is not fair and we all will suffer injustices in life.

One area where we don't expect to see injustice in is in our judicial system. Sadly, there seems to be a problem in our judicial system because if you are politically connected, have the money to hire a high-priced attorney, or are a sports or Hollywood star, you can get away with committing crimes. Many people know that if they committed the same acts that many public figures commit, they would have been locked up from the very beginning. The injustice that happens in our judicial system is truly breaking down our society.

Satan knows that he can destroy a society if he can cause the judiciary to be unjust in their rulings. A society becomes corrupt when money, popularity and position helps someone get out of paying for their crime. There is no justifiable or scriptural reason for anyone to be able to get away with wrong just because they have the money to buy their way out.

Sadly, the same injustice that happens in society seems to have crept into Christianity. A lack of justice is nothing new. We see it happening in the Scriptures with Eli. 1 Samuel 3:13

shows how Eli allowed injustice when God says, *"For I have told him that I will judge his house for ever for the iniquity which he knoweth; because his sons made themselves vile, and he restrained them not."* Sadly, Samuel didn't seem to learn this lesson. 1 Samuel 8:3 says about Samuel's sons, *"And his sons walked not in his ways, but turned aside after lucre, and took bribes, and perverted judgment."* Israel eventually demanded a king because they wanted to do away with the injustice that they saw going on in the spiritual realm that was influencing their society.

The injustice that Eli and Samuel allowed can also destroy a church if sin or infractions of the rules are not dealt with properly. The quickest way to destroy a church's spirit of unity is for the leadership to make decisions based on how it affects their family or church finances. Many pastors have hurt the spirit of other Christians because they've made judgments based on how it affects their family or an influential church family instead of basing their decisions on right and wrong.

Situation ethics is always the precursor to injustice. When you take away the absolutes that God demands, you create a society as seen in the Book of Judges where *"every man did that which was right in his own eyes."* (Judges 17:6) Being just in how you handle every situation is the only way to do away with injustice. Let me give you several principles on being just in your handling of all situations.

1. What does the Word of God say to do?

The first action you should always take when it comes to making decisions is to find out what the Word of God says.

The Word of God is our final and supreme authority. If we don't base our decisions on the Word of God, we will find ourselves using faulty measurements in making decisions on handling a difficult situation which always leads to injustice. Matthew 22:29 says, *"Jesus answered and said unto them, Ye do err, not knowing the scriptures, nor the power of God."* All error in judgment happens when we stop using the Scriptures for our measurement of right and wrong. The purity of God's Word is found in Psalm 12:6 which says, *"The words of the LORD are pure words: as silver tried in a furnace of earth, purified seven times."*

God's Word is the only guiding factor which keeps us from unjust decisions. Psalm 119:11 says, *"Thy word have I hid in mine heart, that I might not sin against thee."* What is it that keeps us from sin? It is the Word of God that keeps anyone from making wrong decisions. If God's Word is what keeps us from making the wrong decisions, we should go to it for every decision we make so that an injustice is not committed.

2. Take feelings out of all personal rulings.

Proverbs 3:1 says, *"My son, forget not my law; but let thine heart keep my commandments:"* This verse is teaching the importance of removing your feelings from decision making and rulings concerning people. You will notice that the law, which is God's Word, is to be the basis by which you make decisions or rulings about people. When you allow your feelings to get involved, you will either rule too harshly or be too lenient. Feelings make decisions based on the emotion of the moment. If you are going to be just, you must remove your feelings out of every decision and ruling you make.

Justice doesn't have feelings because justice is based on right or wrong. If you are going to be just in all your decisions with people, you must take your feelings and emotions out of your decision-making.

3. Listen to both sides before coming to a conclusion.

Deuteronomy 19:15 says, *"One witness shall not rise up against a man for any iniquity, or for any sin, in any sin that he sinneth: at the mouth of two witnesses, or at the mouth of three witnesses, shall the matter be established."* This verse is teaching the importance of hearing all sides of a story. You will always find yourself having to clean up a mess when you make a decision based on one side of a story. Proverbs 18:13 warns, *"He that answereth a matter before he heareth it, it is folly and shame unto him."* God wants you to slow down in making opinions and rulings about situations before you hear both sides of the story. If you come to a conclusion before you allow the other side to tell how they perceive their situation, you will eventually make an unjust ruling. Why? Because, *"He that is first in his own cause seemeth just..."* (Proverbs 18:17) If you are going to be just in all that you do, you better learn to become a person who gets the whole story before you allow your mind to begin deliberation on the matter.

4. Let past dealings dictate present judgments.

Deuteronomy 1:17 says, *"Ye shall not respect persons in judgment; but ye shall hear the small as well as the great; ye shall not be afraid of the face of man; for the judgment is God's: and the cause that is too hard for you, bring it unto me, and I will hear it."* You will notice that justice is treating everyone the same. If you are going to be just in your dealings with people, you better research how you decided to do something in the past before making a decision in the present.

One of the pastors I served under in the past often said, "Let me see what I did in the past about this before I can tell you what I can do." He was trying to be just in his decision. You will become highly respected by those whom you lead if you learn to make all decisions using the same rule. When you start changing your decisions based on the person you are dealing with, you will hurt the trust of those who follow you.

5. Be a person of absolutes.

If you are going to be just in how you deal with people, you must become a person of absolutes. You cannot be just and have gray areas of life. Indecision due to gray areas always creates an atmosphere for injustice. Absolutes always set a person free. John 8:32 says, *"And ye shall know the truth, and the truth shall make you free."* If truth, which never changes, makes you free, then anything that is not an absolute is unjust. The best way to be just with people is to let the absolutes of the Scriptures guide your decisions.

6. Recuse yourself from decisions when you have family and feelings involved.

One of the greatest mistakes many leaders make is in not recusing themselves when their family is involved. I know that every leader thinks they can take their feelings out, but they can't. Eli and Samuel were both very good men, but even they couldn't deal with their family when they were doing wrong. It is hard to be just when your family is involved in the situation. The best thing you can do to be sure that justice is served is to recuse yourself from ruling on a situation and allow another person who is just to make those rulings in your stead.

7. Don't play favorites.

Leaders must be careful not to have favorites. James 2:1 warns, *"My brethren, have not the faith of our Lord Jesus Christ, the Lord of glory, with respect of persons."* God knew that injustices will incur when you start respecting one person above another. This is hard for any leader to do because we are humans, and humans tend to gravitate towards those who treat them in a good manner. However, if you become a person who plays favorites, you will quickly find yourself making decisions that favor those you like over those you don't particularly like. If you are going to be just in your dealings with people, you must avoid having favorites. When people you lead know that if they can persuade a person to influence you because you are closer to them, you have lost the ability to be just in your rulings. You must be as firm on one as you are another. There is no favoritism in just rulings.

8. Rule on each decision the same way you would want someone to rule on a decision if it concerned you or your family.

One of the easiest ways to be just is to rule by how you would want another person to rule with your family. Matthew 7:12 says, *"Therefore all things whatsoever ye would that* men should do to you, do ye even so to them: for this is the law and the prophets."* This verse is commonly known as the Golden Rule. God is teaching that you should treat everyone the same way you would want yourself or your family to be treated.

I believe most people simply want their family to be treated justly. If someone in their family is wrong, the Christian will want their family member to justly pay for their wrong. However, what will cause most people to get angry is when they know their family member is being treated unfairly or differently from others. The best way to be just is to treat everyone the same way you would want others to treat you or your family.

9. Never allow money to influence your decision.

James chapter two deals with the importance of not allowing people with money to influence your decisions. Money cannot be a driving factor in why you make decisions, because if people of money influence your decisions, you will end up favoring them over those with no money. Remember, *"For the love of money is the root of all evil…"* (1 Timothy 6:10)

10. Never allow position to influence your decision.

Proverbs 25:6-7 says, *"Put not forth thyself in the presence of the king, and stand not in the place of great men: For better it is that it be said unto thee, Come up hither; than that thou shouldest be put lower in the presence of the prince whom thine eyes have seen."* If you are going to be just with people, you must never let their position in society influence your treatment of them.

The flesh tends to treat those in authority better than it treats others. The reason is because the flesh knows that if they are in favor with an authority, the authority will probably favor the one who treats them favorably.

You must always keep the mentality that it doesn't matter who is right or wrong, all must be treated the same. Whether it is the authority that is wrong or the children that are wrong, they both must be treated justly. Let me bring this a step further. You should also not hold authority or their children to a higher standard just because of their position. Justice expects everyone to be treated the same no matter the position they hold.

11. Don't rule when you don't know what is the right thing to do.

James 1:8 says, *"A double minded man is unstable in all his ways."* The worst thing to do when dealing with people is to make a ruling when you don't know the right thing to do. Justice makes decisions on absolutes. Doubt is not an absolute; therefore, a decision made in doubt is often a decision that will later be regretted.

What should you do when you don't know what to do? James 1:5 says, *"If any of you lack wisdom, let him ask of God, that giveth to all men liberally, and upbraideth not; and it shall be given him."* When in doubt, always go to God and ask Him to give you the wisdom to clear up the doubt. It is always better to delay a decision so you can be just than to make a quick decision that ends up being unjust. You will never regret taking time to get God's wisdom concerning a situation when seeking justice.

12. Realize that today's ruling will be the measurement for all future rulings.

Matthew 7:1-2 says, *"Judge not, that ye be not judged. For with what judgment ye judge, ye shall be judged: and with what measure ye mete, it shall be measured to you again."* One of the greatest reasons you need to be just in your treatment of others is so that when you are being accused, others will use your measurement of justice to judge you. Everyone is going to be judged at some point. If you are unjust in your dealings with others, you will often find them judging you unjustly.

My friend, justice should start with the Christian. Christians should never lower themselves to the injustices of society. If you don't like how society is unjust, don't be unjust yourself. When you treat everyone justly, you are showing the importance of truth being preeminent in every situation. When truth becomes the measurement for rulings and treatment of people, God's Word will be relevant to all because the Scriptures are truth.

CHAPTER 9

ENTITLEMENTS
THE ATTACK AGAINST WORK ETHICS

"Son, if you want a car, get a job and buy one." This is what my father told me when I was a teenager wanting my own car. I wasn't asking my dad to buy me a car, but he was just making it clear that if I wanted a car, I was going to have to work so I would have the money to pay for the insurance and gas.

My dad often said to me about working, "If there's nothing to do, pick up a broom and sweep the floor." He understood that I would never advance at any job if I stood around waiting for someone else to do my job.

I can remember when I was a boy that I saw many of my friend's parents give them an allowance every week. One day I went to my dad and asked him why they didn't give me an allowance. My father responded by saying, "Your allowance is that you get to eat the food off our table and sleep in a bed we paid for." Certainly, my parents could have given me one dollar a week if they wanted, but they were teaching me that money is not free. They wanted me to understand that I was not entitled to money and that if I wanted it, I needed to work for it.

These were just a few of the statements my parents said to teach me the scriptural principle of working for what I wanted or needed instead of looking for a handout. The result of my parents teaching me these principles is the satisfaction that everything I have today I worked for and purchased myself. Their wisdom in teaching me the fallacy of having an entitlement mentality keeps me from looking for everyone else to pay my way instead of working hard so that I can have the money for what I need or want.

One of the greatest mistakes America made was when it legislated the requirement of a work permit for any child under 16 years of age. I'm sure those who put this piece of legislation together meant well, but it has greatly contributed to many children not learning the rewards of working and learning a good work ethic at a young age. The entitlement mentality that we see today is a direct result of parents giving their children everything they want instead of teaching them to work for it.

We live in times when many young people expect everyone else to do something for them instead of finding a way to work for what they want. Who would have ever thought that young people would actually sue their parents because their parents wouldn't pay for their college tuition? This is ludicrous! Too many young people think that life owes them, and instead of finding a job and working hard, they live off government entitlements and never learn the rewards of working hard.

Another reason so many have the entitlement mentality is because their parents have given them everything. Parents don't want their children to have to "suffer" like they did when they were young, so instead of making their children work, they give them everything. By giving their children everything, parents create an entitlement mentality in their children.

The Scriptures are very clear that you should work for what you get. 2 Thessalonians 3:10 says, *"For even when we were with you, this we commanded you, that if any would not work, neither should he eat."* God's principle of working is clear when you see that He didn't give Israel the Promised Land without having to work for it. God told Israel that the Promised Land was theirs to have, but they were going to have to conquer the inhabitants of the land and rebuild the cities after taking it.

From the very beginning of Creation, God established the principle of having a work ethic. Genesis 2:15 shows this when it says, *"And the LORD God took the man, and put him into the garden of Eden to dress it and to keep it."* You will notice that God created the Earth, but Adam was to work to dress it and keep it. God did His part in creating the world, but He knew that Adam would not be happy unless he worked every day.

After Adam and Eve sinned, God drove them out of the garden of Eden. God told Adam after driving them out *"...to till the ground from whence he was taken."* (Genesis 3:23) God always commanded man to work for everything he was to receive.

The entitlement mentality that so many push is an attack against God's principle of working for what you get. God knows that working makes a person happy, but Satan also knows that entitlements eventually lead to an anti-God society.

All you have to do is look at every society where government entitlements are given, and you will see a society where God has a very little part in those societies. The Scriptures give us several observations about entitlements and work.

1. Nothing is truly free; somebody has to pay for it.

I was entering a hotel in Virginia to go to my room when I saw two young men watching a political rally on the television. I walked over to them and saw President Trump, at that time he was just a candidate, giving a speech. I asked the young men what they thought about him, and they responded negatively.

I then thought I would find out who they wanted to be president and why. The person they wanted to be president was promising free college tuition. I asked the young men why they wanted this person to be president and they responded, "Because he wants to give us free tuition for college." I asked the young men who was going to pay for this. I then began to tell them that somebody had to pay for the teacher's salaries, electric bills, building maintenance and so forth. I told them that free might sound good, but somebody still has to pay for it and that they should pay their own way instead of expecting someone else to pay it for them. Of course, this didn't sit well with these young men and they walked off in disgust.

The fact is that everything has a price. Even if someone gives you something, they still have to pay for it. Look at salvation; it is a gift, but Jesus paid for it with His life and blood. Romans 6:23 says, *"For the wages of sin is death; but the gift* of God is eternal life through Jesus Christ our Lord." Just like Jesus had to pay for our salvation, everything you want in life has a price. You are not entitled to salvation, and you are not entitled to everything you want in life. There is a price for everything, and the only way to pay that price is to work for it.

2. An entitlement mentality leads to a faithless mindset.

The entitlement mentality has the mindset that someone other than God should give them everything they want. Philippians 4:19 shows us differently when it says, *"But my God shall supply all your need according to his riches in glory by Christ Jesus."* God supplies your need, but He supplies it by giving you a job to earn money.

When others pay your way, you stop living by faith. The Christian life is to be a life that is lived by faith with complete dependence upon God by faith. Hebrews 11:6 says, *"But without faith it is impossible to please him: for he that cometh to God must believe that he is, and that he is a rewarder of them that diligently seek him."*

Any Christian who lives off entitlements will not live by faith because faith requires work. When I stepped out by faith into evangelism, it required me to work to make it. Yes, God supplied my needs, but He supplied them by allowing me to work for what I received. You will never live by faith when you are expecting everyone else to pay your way.

3. An entitlement mentality is a selfish attitude.

One thing you will learn about those who feel they are entitled to everything is that they are very selfish individuals.

There was a young man in Matthew 19 who thought he was entitled to salvation, and the Scriptures show us his selfish mindset. You can see his mindset in verses 21-22 where it says, *"Jesus said unto him, If thou wilt be perfect, go and sell that thou hast, and give to the poor, and thou shalt have treasure in heaven: and come and follow me. But when the young man heard that saying, he went away sorrowful: for he had great possessions."* His entitled mindset led him to go away sorrowful because his selfishness didn't get what it wanted.

Christian, nobody is owed anything. If we got what we deserved, we would get Hell because of the payment for sin. Instead of seeking to get what we want, we should be seeking to meet the needs of others. 1 Corinthians 10:24 says, *"Let no man seek his own, but every man another's wealth."* If you continue living as if you deserve everything, you will continue to be disappointed with life. An entitlement mentality always leads to a sorrowful life because you will not always get what you want. At some point the entitlements will stop, and at that point is when you will be disappointed.

4. An entitlement mentality leads to a dependency on government instead of a dependency on God.

The entitlement mentality is nothing short of idolatry. Exodus 20:3 says, *"Thou shalt have no other gods before me."* When you depend on anyone other than God, then whatever you depend upon has become your god. Eventually, people cannot give you everything; thus, that is when you begin to depend on government for what you want. My friend, this is idolatry.

Moreover, when you depend on the government to give you what you want, the government will be able to make you do what it wants you to do, and you won't have a choice in the matter. I look at how Egyptians went to Joseph in their famine and depended on the government to pay their way. When the government owned everything they had, you will find that Joseph controlled the people. Look at what happened in Exodus 47:21, *"And as for the people, he removed them to cities from one end of the borders of Egypt even to the other end thereof."* The people no longer had the freedom to do what they wanted to do because they became an entitled society which led to the government dictating what they could and could not do, and where they could and could not live. Likewise, when the Christian embraces the entitlement mentality, they will no longer be able to follow God's guidance in their life because whoever they depend upon for their entitlement controls where they can go and what they can do.

5. Entitlement mentality leads to laziness.

The end road of an entitlement society is a lazy society. If you can get what you want without having to work for it, you become lazy and dependent on others. Proverbs 13:4 shows us the end of laziness when it says, *"The soul of the sluggard desireth, and hath nothing: but the soul of the diligent shall be made fat."* Once you become lazy, you never get what you want because you always have to depend on others to get it for you.

If we are going to overcome the entitlement society, we are going to have to acquire a good work ethic. There are several things about working that you need to learn so that you can acquire a good work ethic.

1. Work is meant to be hard.

A young man came to me and told me that he was going to quit his job. I asked him why he wanted to quit his job. His response was, "The job where I work is hard." I couldn't believe what I had just heard because I have always been taught to work hard.

When I was growing up, my parents never let me complain about how hard a task was because they were teaching me that work is meant to be hard. At age thirteen, I started picking strawberries for ten hours a day every summer. Though none of my friends lasted in the fields, I worked in the strawberry fields for three summers until I was old enough to start working at a paper factory. Though picking strawberries was hard, I never thought anything about it because I knew that work was supposed to be hard.

Genesis 3:19 says, *"In the sweat of thy face shalt thou eat bread, till thou return unto the ground..."* You must stop looking for easy work and just accept that work is going to be hard. If you always look for the easy job, you will eventually accept the entitlements given because it is easier to sit on a couch and get a check, but you will never be satisfied with yourself.

2. Man should work more than rest.

We live in times when people are trying to find more ways to get out of work than they are trying to find ways to work.

God set the standard for how much we should work in creation. Exodus 20:9 says, *"Six days shalt thou labour, and do all thy work:"* I'm not against people taking time off to rest, but I believe we have gotten to a point where people want to play more than they desire to work. God ordained man to work for six days. I believe you will feel better about yourself when you follow God's standard for working. Instead of trying to get out of work, you need to find ways to work. Working people are always happy people.

3. Working hard helps you to sleep better.

One of the best benefits of working hard is having a good nights rest. Ecclesiastes 5:12 says, *"The sleep of a labouring man is sweet, whether he eat little or much…"* The best way to fight insomnia is to work hard. I have found that the harder I work, the better I sleep. My wife will often tell me that I slept hard the night before. Every time she tells me that, I look back to how hard I worked that day, and it never fails that it was a long day of working. Entitled people tend to stay up late and sleep in late, which only feeds their lazy character. If you work hard, you will find you won't have any problems sleeping at night.

4. Children should be taught to work before play.

One of the greatest mistakes that parents make is allowing their children to play before they do their chores. Children should always be required to work before they play. I know that sometimes it is easier just to let your children play so you can get done what you wanted them to do, but you are teaching them a bad habit that will lead them to feel entitled.

Nobody should play or eat without working first. You can start your children's day off working by requiring them to make their bed before they can eat breakfast. They may not like this, but you are teaching them the importance of work before pleasure.

A pleasure mentality without working always leads to sin. Exodus 32:6 shows us that Israel lost its work ethic when they built the golden calf. This verse says about them, *"And they rose up early on the morrow, and offered burnt offerings, and brought peace offerings; and the people sat down to eat and to drink, and rose up to play."* The best way to keep your children from getting into trouble is by making them work. If they work hard every day, they will be too tired to get themselves into trouble.

5. Working makes you more like God.

Finally, the best thing about working is that it is a God-like character trait. God worked six days in creation, and only rested on the seventh. If you want to be more like God, the best way to do that is to go work. Stop waiting for everyone to give you something, stop looking for handouts, and get the right mentality by working for what you get. When you acquire the mentality to work, you will have a greater respect for God and His principles for living.

Chapter 10

TEARING DOWN HISTORY

There has been a concerted effort on the left to fundamentally change who we are as Americans. Little by little they have gone after the core of America's soul in an attempt to move God right out of our country. They have done so with their battle against prayer in the public schools, and by removing God's Word from any and all government entities including our public schools. They have tried to continue to change who we are by teaching evolution as a fact when it is only a false theory. They have tried to belittle any semblance of religion so they can turn the eyes of Americans away from God.

One of the greater ways they are trying to change the soul of America is being propagated by the social justice warriors who are trying to remove any statue of those in history whom they deem as slave owners. Of course, the initial personality they have gone after is General Robert E. Lee. Because General Lee led the Confederate armies, they have led a concerted effort to tear down all statues that have been erected in his honor. Their supposed contention is that he was for slavery because that is what they have said the Civil War was about. Again, the left has done a good job in changing history through our public education system. Though Abraham Lincoln used slavery as a tool to rally the North, the real reason for the Civil War was states rights, not slavery. Because most people have learned the wrong reason for the Civil War, they can easily be swayed to think that

General Lee didn't care for those who were slaves; therefore, many think it is just to tear down every statue in Lee's honor to cleanse ourselves of this portion of history.

What many don't understand is that the agenda of the social justice warriors goes far deeper than General Lee. Their ultimate goal is to change the Constitution. They know that the Constitution found most, if not all, of its principles in the Scriptures, and the only way they can change America is to change our Constitution. Well, they've found a way to do it by tearing down history. If these people have their way with General Lee, they will eventually go after every American forefather who had a part in the founding of these United States. Once they go after our forefathers, they will contend that the founding documents of our nation are tainted by slave owners; therefore. we must change our Constitution to fit our "enlightened" society. You can doubt me on this if you want, but this is the ultimate goal of these people. The Constitution is our basis as to what we believe as Americans, and until they can change it, they will not be able to fundamentally change who we are as a nation.

The purpose of tearing down history is to change the core Christian beliefs of this nation to fit their Godless lifestyles. All you have to do to change the core beliefs of a people is to change their history because history teaches us who we are and why we are this way. The importance of telling the true story of our history is to teach us the founding principles of this nation which are a direct result of God's Word.

Sadly, the attempt to tear down history has also fallen into our independent Baptist ranks. There is a concerted effort by many to criticize those whom God used in previous generations to build great independent, fundamental Baptist churches with Scriptural standards. It is easy to sit and criticize them because their lives are now history and we can see the mistakes they made; however, if these people are successful in tearing down those who gave us what we have, they will continue to go all the way back to Peter and Paul. I know that many are rolling their eyes right now, but the attempt to pull out the Pauline epistles is already trying to make its way into our Baptist movement. If these progressive, backslidden or lost people are successful in tearing down our history, they will eventually attack the King James Bible and say it is tainted because our forefathers are the ones whom God used to pass it down to this generation.

Satan's attack has always been against God's Word, and his tool to destroy God's Word is by tearing down history. When Satan challenged Eve to eat of the forbidden fruit, he did so by attacking the veracity of history. Satan said in Genesis 3:1, *"...Yea, hath God said..."* Yes, Satan was attacking God's Word by questioning it, but in reality he was trying to tear down history to make Eve believe that she knew better than God's Word. Satan showed his disdain for Eve's belief in God's Word, which was her history, by saying in verses 3-4, *"And the serpent said unto the woman, Ye shall not surely die: For God doth know that in the day ye eat thereof, then your eyes shall be opened, and ye shall be as gods, knowing good and evil."* Satan wanted God out of the picture, so the only way he could do this was by tearing down Eve's history. God's Word was her history and core of what she believed.

What was the result of destroying her history? The result was heartache and sorrow. The ground was cursed because they disobeyed God by ignoring their history. *"Thorns also and thistles"* were the result of ignoring how history taught them to live. The result is found in Romans 5:8 which says, *"Wherefore, as by one man sin entered into the world, and death by sin; and so death passed upon all men, for that all have sinned:"* Death is always the result of tearing down history. If they had just listened to God and obeyed His Word, the destruction this world has faced would have never happened.

My friend, our history is important to who we are, what we believe, and to our children's future. If we allow the social justice warriors to win in rewriting the history of our nation and the independent, fundamental, Baptist movement so they can justify their sinful and worldly lifestyles, we will succeed in destroying the future of our children. Psalm 33:12 reminds us, *"Blessed is the nation whose God is the LORD; and the people whom he hath chosen for his own inheritance."* The greatest reason God has blessed America is because God has been our LORD. Likewise, the reason God has blessed the independent, fundamental Baptists is because we have made God our sole authority on all that we do and say. If we tear down our history, we will destroy the source of God's blessings. Several things we must beware of about history.

1. You can always find flaws.

You don't have to look hard at history to find that those whom we look to for examples have made mistakes, and some of those mistakes were big ones. The only reason you are going to find mistakes is because everyone is a sinner. Just because you have found a mistake doesn't mean that we should erase all the good things they passed down to us. If history's flaws should cause us not to follow anything they gave us, then we should be sure never to read any of the Psalms because David certainly made some huge mistakes. Likewise, we should also throw out the Pauline epistles because Paul made the mistake of taking a Jewish vow when he knew that it was wrong. Certainly, we should take out the Pentateuch because Moses murdered a man and also smote the rock when he was supposed to speak to it. We also might consider removing the books of Peter considering that the Apostle Peter denied Christ.

As ridiculous as it would be to remove these books from God's Word, it is just as ridiculous for us to remove the influence of those from the past who handed the independent, fundamental Baptist movement to us. Yes, those in the past who were leaders in the independent Baptist movement had flaws, but nobody ever said they were perfect. It is easy to sit in criticism of these in history because the book of their life is written; however, let me caution you that the book of your life is still being written. The next generation is going to find flaws in your life as well. I am not saying that we worship those from the past, but their influence is important to who we are and what we do.

2. History's flaws are not an excuse for worldly living.

Just because you discovered the flaws of those from the past doesn't give you an excuse to live like the world.

Jeroboam made this mistake after the young prophet who delivered God's message to him disobeyed and was killed by God. 1 Kings 13:33 says, *"After this thing Jeroboam returned not from his evil way..."* Jeroboam used the disobedience of this prophet as his excuse to do wrong. However, God showed what He thought about this in verse 34 when He said, *"And this thing became sin unto the house of Jeroboam, even to cut it off, and to destroy it from off the face of the earth."*

It doesn't matter how wrong someone in the past may have been, it doesn't change the good they accomplished, and it doesn't give you a right to dress worldly, listen to the world's music, and to drink beer and wine. Using the sins of the past generation as your excuse to live like the world is evil, sinful, and rebellious.

3. History's flaws should be building blocks, not tools of criticism.

One of the reasons God gave us the whole story of the characters in the Scriptures is so that we can learn what not to do. God never intended for us to sit and criticize them. 1 Corinthians 10:11 teaches this when it says, *"Now all these things happened unto them for ensamples: and they are written for our admonition, upon whom the ends of the world are come."*

Just because we may not like some of the flaws that we have discovered about those in history doesn't give us a right to be critical of every move they made. My friend, instead of sitting with the magnifying glass trying to find another reason to blame the fundamental Baptist world for people going bad, why don't you instead use those flaws as building blocks of what to avoid in your life. History can either be a weapon to criticize, or it can be a tool to learn how to better reach the lost without changing who we are as Christians.

4. Your view of history will become your history.

What you view as the flaws of history will ultimately determine what your history becomes. If you change everything you do to prove history wrong, you will change who you are in the present. You have to understand that every action you take is making up your history. You may try to right all the wrongs of history, but the only thing you are doing is changing who we are for the next generation. You better be careful about trying to change history, because it is ultimately the tool Satan uses to get us to change the Word of God.

5. Your treatment of history is teaching the next generation how to treat history.

The next generation is watching what you do with those who walked before you. They are learning from you how to treat those in their history. One of the admonitions Paul gave in 2 Thessalonians 2:15 was, *"Therefore, brethren, stand fast, and hold the traditions which ye have been taught, whether by word, or our epistle."* You are writing an epistle to be read by the next generation. Matthew 7:12 warns, *"...whatsoever ye would that men should do to you, do ye even so to them..."* If you want the next generation to treat you and what you have done for the LORD right, you had better be sure to treat the next generation right for they are learning from you.

6. Tearing down history is done with little steps.

History is not destroyed all at once; it is destroyed little by little. Samson was not destroyed all at once; he was destroyed little by little. It is interesting that his final destruction came through the hands of Delilah. Delilah wasn't a mighty warrior, but she was a languishing woman who was used by the enemy to destroy Samson.

Song of Solomon 2:15 says, *"Take us the foxes, the little foxes, that spoil the vines..."* Notice that the little foxes destroy the vines of history. The enemy doesn't try to take everything at one time; instead, they take a little bit of history at a time by causing good people to be critical of it instead of learning from it.

7. If you don't change history, you can change history.

One of the things I have learned in life is that the lessons we learn from history can help us to do greater works if we don't sit in criticism. Certainly, there were no faults in Jesus, but even He said in John 14:12, *"...greater works than these shall he do; because I go unto my Father."*

God gave us the lessons from history so that we could move on from where they were to do greater works for the LORD. I often tell people that my ministry should do more than my parents because I have the wisdom from their lives to build on. If I tear down everything from history and rebuild from where I am, I am wasting the foundations that all the previous generations have built upon so that I can do greater works for the LORD.

8. Every generation is to pass unchanged history to the next generation.

2 Thessalonians 2:15 says, *"Therefore, brethren, stand fast, and hold the traditions which ye have been taught, whether by word, or our epistle."* What are these *"traditions?"* It is the history that has been handed down to us from previous generations. These traditions are lessons that the previous generations learned how to do the LORD's work and how to live to please the LORD. Our job is not to change our beliefs, but to teach them so that the next generation will continue to teach them to their next generation.

If you tear down history, you will keep the next generation from learning the traditions that are beneficial to help us to live for the LORD. One reason we shouldn't change history as we pass it down is because it enables the next generation to learn from the mistakes of past generations as well as learn from their victories, and both are equally important. Picking and choosing from what you don't like about the previous generation only leads to Swiss cheese Christianity that has holes all through it. Christian, the best thing you can do is to *"hold the traditions"* and not criticize them and change them.

9. The changes you make now are the doctrine for the next generation.

The danger of tearing down history is that what we teach today becomes the foundations for the next generation to build upon. When truth is no longer passed down to the next generation, then lies become the truth for the next generation to build upon. Yes, I know that we are to stay focused on Christ, but even the Scriptures talk about *"the foundation of the apostles and prophets, Jesus Christ himself being the chief corner stone;"* (Ephesians 2:20) Your responsibility is to be sure the foundations of the old paths, independent Baptist movement are not changed. Always remember that the old paths never change, but they can be forgotten because progressive Baptists don't want to pay the price to keep those paths obvious for the next generation to walk down. We are always one generation away from losing the foundations of the old paths. It is your responsibility to be sure the next generation is handed what has been handed to you.

10. Every time you change history, you are ultimately attacking God's Word.

Ultimately it comes down to this; the tearing down of history is to get us to accept that the King James Bible is not the Word of God. That may not be your goal, but that is the goal of those to whom you are listening who criticize our history. Just like Satan got Eve to sin by considering his questioning of history, he is trying to get you to question the history of the old paths and blame them for all the problems.

The old paths are not the problem; sin is the problem. The old paths have always led us to the blessings of God. The problems you see in our history have nothing to do with the old paths, but everything to do with the sin of some of those who used to walk those paths. Instead of tearing down history, you would be wise to fight sin and keep what has been handed to you the same. The enemy will cause you to become disenfranchised with history for the sake of getting you to tear it down. Don't let your dislike of the actions of those in history cause you to tear down what has been handed to you. If you allow it to be torn down, you will not like the results it gives. We know where the old paths lead, and we also know that these new paths of history are leading to heartache. Always remember that those in history who sinned had to leave the old paths to commit their sin.

My friend, fight sin, but leave history alone. History has valuable lessons to teach, and ultimately God's Word is our history. If we start tearing down history, others will keep going until they get to the foundation of what we believe which is God's Word.

CHAPTER 11

INCLUSIVE TOLERANCE
THE MEGA-VOICE OF LIBERALS

I'm always amused at how liberals demand that conservatives allow them to come to the bargaining table when the conservative is in power. Yet, when the liberal is in power they never one time ask the conservative for their opinion, nor do they ask them to come to the bargaining table. Instead, they demand that we conform to their way of thinking. The liberal is always demanding that the conservative tone down their rhetoric, but it is always amazing how the liberal can say anything they want and do anything they want, and that is considered acceptable.

For instance, a sodomite couple in Colorado demanded of a bakery to bake a wedding cake for them. It didn't matter to these sodomites that there were other bakeries that would have happily baked them a cake. Instead, they went to the one bakery they knew would not bake them a cake because they were Christians, and they took them to court saying that this shop discriminated against them. News pundits everywhere were aghast that this bakery wouldn't bake a cake for this sinful couple. They said that the owners of this bakery needed to be inclusive and tolerant of lifestyles that were in direct contradiction to their personal beliefs.

However, it is interesting that the inclusive tolerant groups never one time were inclusive of those who believe that this is a chosen and abominable lifestyle. Why is it that they demand for those of us who believe this lifestyle is wrong to change and they don't have to change themselves? Their hypocrisy reveals that they are not interested in being inclusive or tolerant, but they are only interested in those of us who don't believe like they do conforming to their way of thinking.

The same hypocrisy is seen with liberals who demand that women be given equal rights, or that black people be considered equal to white people. Yet, when a woman or a black man who is conservative makes sure that their conservative voice is heard, the same liberals call these good people words that this author will not repeat.

My question to these liberals who are so interested in inclusive tolerance, where is your tolerance for the conservative? Where is your tolerance for those of us who believe that abortion is murder? Where is your tolerance for the conservative black movement? Where is your tolerance for conservative ladies who have acquired powerful positions? Where is your tolerance for the Christian who exercises their right to free speech by witnessing on the streets? Where is your tolerance for people who want to put up a nativity scene at Christmas? Where is your tolerance for those who believe it is wise to pray for the safety of players before sporting events? Could it be that liberals are not truly interested in inclusivity or tolerance, but rather they are interested in forcing us to conform to their wicked and evil lifestyles?

Romans 12:2 make it clear that the Christian is not to conform to inclusive tolerance when it says, *"And be not conformed to this world: but be ye transformed by the renewing of your mind, that ye may prove what is that good, and acceptable, and perfect, will of God."* God didn't say to be conformed to the wicked lifestyles of the world; rather, the Christian is to transform their mind to think like Christ.

Sadly, the inclusive tolerant movement has crept into Christianity. There are many people today who think we must be tolerant of worldly lifestyles and not be so "divisive" with the brethren over so called "minor" issues. Let me remind you that God commands the Christian in 2 Corinthians 6:17, *"Wherefore come out from among them, and be ye separate, saith the Lord, and touch not the unclean thing; and I will receive you,"* The inclusive tolerant movement from progressive Christian leaders is nothing more than a call to compromise. Any Christian who says that Christians should be more tolerant of the world is a Christian who does not love the LORD the way they should. James 4:4 shows this when it says, *"Ye adulterers and adulteresses, know ye not that the friendship of the world is enmity with God? whosoever therefore will be a friend of the world is the enemy of God."* There is no way that inclusive tolerance can be the way of life for a Christian and that Christian still be right with the LORD.

The call for inclusive tolerance is not a new movement. The Scriptures are full of instances when the world demanded that God's people become more inclusive and tolerant of their ways. One of the main instances where we see the demand for God's people to be inclusive and tolerant of wickedness was when Pharaoh demanded Moses to compromise his beliefs to accept Egypt's way of worship. Yet, each time Pharaoh offered a compromise, God told Moses to refuse it

INCLUSIVE TOLERANCE

because God wanted Israel to serve Him exclusively outside of the camp of Egypt.

You may recall how Sanballat and Geshem sent a message to Nehemiah which said, *"Come, let us meet together in some one of the villages in the plain of Ono."* (Nehemiah 6:2) When Nehemiah received the request, he saw that they intended to harm the work being done. Nehemiah responded properly when he said in verse 3, *"...I am doing a great work, so that I cannot come down: why should the work cease, whilst I leave it, and come down to you?"* Nehemiah's response is the exact response that every Christian should have when it comes to the world's or the liberal's call to be inclusive and tolerant of their lifestyle.

The inclusive tolerant group's demand is always that we sit down at the bargaining table to figure out a compromise so that we can all get along. The problem is that the Christian must never get along with sin. The thought that a Christian entertains sin is simply ludicrous. Let me give you several thoughts on why the Christian should never consider the compromise to be inclusive and tolerant of the world and its lifestyle.

1. The first to move always loses.

The story in 1 Kings 20 that tells how Benhadad, the King of Syria, sent messengers to Ahab to give him all the gold, silver, his wives, and every possession to him or he would come and kill him. This threat shook Ahab so much that he responded by saying in verse 4, *"My lord, O king, according to thy saying, I am thine, and all that I have."* Ahab thought that moving a little would appease Benhadad and cause him to leave Israel alone.

Ahab found out the hard way that the first move dictated to Benhadad that he would move again. Verses 5-6 say, *"And the messengers came again, and said, Thus speaketh Benhadad, saying, Although I have sent unto thee, saying, Thou shalt deliver me thy silver, and thy gold, and thy wives, and thy children; Yet I will send my servants unto thee to morrow about this time, and they shall search thine house, and the houses of thy servants; and it shall be, that whatsoever is pleasant in thine eyes, they shall put it in their hand, and take it away."* Hold on! I thought Benhadad only wanted the silver and gold. The fact that Ahab moved showed Benhadad that he would move again.

You always have to realize that when you are willing to move one time for the world, they will always demand that you move again. Liberals are always going to say that if you will become a little more tolerant of them that they will gladly meet you in the middle. The problem: they are lying. Liberals always want you to make the first move because they know they don't plan on moving.

2. Tolerance is not a one-way street.

As previously shown in this chapter, liberals will never be tolerant of the Christian lifestyle. As a Christian, I don't expect the world or liberals to like what I do or to tolerate my beliefs because they believe their way is right the same way that I believe the Scriptures are right. Tolerance can never happen. Romans 8:7 clearly shows this to be true when it says,

INCLUSIVE TOLERANCE

"Because the carnal mind is enmity against God: for it is not subject to the law of God, neither indeed can be." You must always remember that tolerance is not a one-way street; it is a dead-end street.

3. God never said to be liked by the world, but He did say to reach the world.

The progressive Christian liberal makes it sound that if we are more tolerant of the world that the world will like us more enabling us to better reach them. This is foolishness to the core! You cannot reach the world when you compromise truth because truth cannot be changed. John 8:32 says, *"And ye shall know the truth, and the truth shall make you free."* The only way for the world to be set free from the bondage of sin is with unfettered truth. If you do right, the world is never going to like you. Luke 21:17 shows this when it says, *"And ye shall be hated of all men for my name's sake."* The fact that we represent God, the enemy of Satan and the world, reveals that no matter what we do the world will never like us. God's command to the Christian is simple, *"I sent you to reap..."* (John 4:38) I am not saying that we have to be a jerk to reach the world, but I am saying we are to preach the Gospel and live according to the Scriptures without compromise or apology.

4. You will always be considered an obstructionist when you won't tolerate sin.

You are always going to have to understand that when you stand for truth and won't consider compromise that you will be considered an obstructionist. Ahab said when he saw

Elijah, *"Art thou he that troubleth Israel?"* (1 Kings 18:17) The enemies of Paul said about him, *"For we have found this man a pestilent fellow, and a mover of sedition among all the Jews throughout the world..."* (Acts 24:5) Herod put John the Baptist in prison and eventually killed him because he told him that his adulterous relationship with his sister-in-law was wrong. Even Paul asked the church in Galatia, *"Am I therefore become your enemy, because I tell you the truth?"* (Galatians 4:16)

Christian, it doesn't matter how nice you are to the world, they will always call you names because they don't want to change how they are living. It is amazing that the ones who adhere to the truth are considered the troublemakers when they haven't changed. You will always have to expect the world to attack you, but never allow their attacks to weary you to the point that you become tolerant of their sin.

5. Compromise always leads to greater sin.

Always remember that what you accept in moderation the next generation will commit in excess. 1 Kings 16:30 says, *"And Ahab the son of Omri did evil in the sight of the LORD above all that were before him."* You will notice that Ahab wasn't the first one to do wrong, but he did more wrong than those before him. The danger of becoming tolerant of sin is that you are telling the next generation that the sin you are tolerating is not bad. Moreover, when you become inclusive of liberals, you are allowing your children to learn the liberal's ways and to meet their children. You can always be guaranteed that if you become tolerant of sin, your children will perceive your tolerance as permission to partake in it.

6. Compromise keeps on taking.

The words from 1 Kings 20:5 will always ring true when you compromise, *"And the messengers came again…"* Once you agree to compromise, you will find that the messengers of compromise will continue to come and demand your tolerance until you totally accept and conform to their sinful lifestyles.

7. An agreement with compromise is always a loss.

Compromise is the departure from truth. If compromise is the departure from truth, that means you departed truth to accept lies. That, my friend, is a total loss. You must realize that you are either doing the work of truth, or you are doing the work of lies. It doesn't matter how many times you have compromised, each time you compromise you lose. Have you ever noticed that those who demand your compromise never keep their word when you move? The messengers of compromise are never going to keep their word because they are trying to shame you into moving by calling you names. You are going to have to get thick skin and ignore the messengers of compromise so that truth doesn't lose.

8. You never recover the ground you lost in compromise.

Ahab never regained the silver and gold he lost when he gave in to Benhadad's demand of compromise. I rarely see those who compromise return to the place where they once stood. Once you lose ground, you may return to a point, but you never go back to the place where you once stood.

One of the greatest reasons you should never give in to compromise is so that the next generation doesn't lose sight of where they should stand. The messengers of compromise take ground from you that you never recover no matter how hard you may try. You must stand firm against the messengers of compromise so that you always keep the stance for truth that you are supposed to keep.

9. You vanish your credibility when you compromise.

Ahab's credibility with his servants was lost the moment he surrendered to the messengers of compromise. Many Christians and men of God who once stood for truth have lost their credibility because they have compromised the message they once used to preach and live. My friend, you may think that people will like you more if you compromise or tolerate their lifestyle, but you will find out that they will lose all respect for you because you moved.

When I was a teenage boy, the men I worked with brought beer to drink during lunch on a day when none of the bosses were present. We were working when one man asked me if I would go and get him a can of beer. I told him that I not only don't drink beer, but I don't touch it either. A couple of days later he told me the reason he asked me to get him a can of beer was because he wanted to see how much I really believed that it was wrong. My credibility was put to the test by that man who I was later able to lead to Christ.

You never know when the world is going to give you a credibility test. One of the reasons you must always do right and never tolerate sin is because you don't want to flunk their credibility test. The world may not like where we stand and what we believe, but if you firmly stand for right, they will respect that you are not willing to move.

10. Compromise is never a faith move.

The problem with compromise is that it is not a forward move, but a backward move. Faith is always going in a forward direction. Hebrews 11:6 reminds us, *"But without faith it is impossible to please him…"* You cannot tolerate sin or compromise your beliefs and be looking forward by faith. Faith always has its eyes on whom it trusts, and if your faith is placed in God, you cannot ever move back by tolerating wrong.

11. We are commanded to contend, not tolerate.

Jude 1:3 tells the Christian to *"earnestly contend for the faith which was once delivered unto the saints."* This verse does not say to earnestly tolerate the world and their lifestyle. Christian, you are either contending for the faith or you are contending against it. When you tolerate sin, you are contending against the faith. When you compromise the truth to be accepted by the world, you are contending against the faith.

12. The Christian is commanded to be steadfast.

God's command to the Christian is found in 1 Corinthians 15:58 when He says, *"Therefore, my beloved brethren, be ye stedfast, unmoveable, always abounding in the work of the Lord, forasmuch as ye know that your labour is not in vain in the Lord."* The Christian is commanded to never move. My friend, the world may cry for tolerance by offering compromise, but God orders the Christian to be *"stedfast, unmoveable."* You may not be liked by the world because you won't move, but you will always please God by standing and being stedfast.

Chapter 12

RESULT-FOCUSED

Several years ago, I watched a roundtable of liberals and conservatives debating whether it was right to slander someone just for the sake of winning an election. It seemed to surprise most of those at the table at the response of the one representing the liberals. He said that it didn't matter to the liberal if what they did was wrong as long as they won. Their focus was on winning and whatever they had to do to win, even if it is lying and destroying someone's character, they would be willing to do it to secure their desired result.

Focusing on the results and not worrying about the consequences has always been the liberal's model. The liberal justifies their actions as long as they get the results they want. The liberal doesn't think that the actions it takes to get the results matter or are wrong as long as they get the desired results.

Winning at any cost is the mindset of liberals, and it is this mindset that will destroy the character of a society. I am all for winning, but losing your soul to gain the world doesn't mean much when you've lost your core beliefs. Jesus asked in Matthew 16:26, *"For what is a man profited, if he shall gain the whole world, and lose his own soul? or what shall a man give in exchange for his soul?"* If you lose your soul in the journey to gain the world, what do you have to say for yourself? The consequences you face tomorrow are just as important as the results you enjoy today. A result-focused society destroys the next generation if they don't look at the consequences of today's actions. Many people have lived to regret the result-focused mentality when they see their children and grandchildren doing things they thought they would never do.

Many parents never thought that making their children work for what they got was important until they saw their children grow up and never take responsibility of paying for themselves. Many parents have grown children living in their homes because they thought it was the compassionate thing to pay their child's way through life instead of making their children work for what they get.

Many people have sold their soul for secular success only to see their children and grandchildren doing things they never imagined they would do. They sold their soul for a secular position, or for more money, but the grave consequences they suffered years after their choice caused them to wish they had never chosen results over future consequences.

In Luke 12:16-21, there was a rich young man who dwelt on the results of today without considering tomorrow's consequences. The rich fool said in verse 19, *"And I will say to my soul, Soul, thou hast much goods laid up for many years; take thine ease, eat, drink, and be merry."* You will notice that his focus was on the immediate. Sadly, there was a verse 20 which says, *"But God said unto him, Thou fool, this night thy soul shall be required of thee…"* This rich fool lived to satisfy the present like many do today only to regret his decision the next day.

RESULT-FOCUSED

In Luke 15, the prodigal son demanded that his father give him the *"portion of goods that falleth to me."* He then went out and *"wasted his substance with riotous living."* This boy never took into consideration the consequences of his decisions. He was only concerned with the present result of living it up in the world and enjoying the lifestyles of society, but he never considered that one day the money his father gave him would all be spent. This prodigal never thought that one day he would desire to eat the slop of the swine. The whole reason he ended up in that condition was because he was result-focused instead of considering the consequences of tomorrow.

After all the good that Hezekiah accomplished, he fell into Satan's trap of living for the immediate results instead of considering the consequences that his actions would bring on the morrow. In his pride, he showed his entire palace and kingdom to the Babylonian spies thinking that it would bring him more prestige among the world leaders. He was so result-focused that after hearing God's judgment upon his children he said, *"Good is the word of the LORD which thou hast spoken. And he said, Is it not good, if peace and truth be in my days?"* (2 Kings 20:19) This mindset led to his children suffering the consequences of his compromise.

What I find disturbing is that many pastors have led their churches to become result-focused instead of truth-focused. Many pastors have compromised what they believe just to build a large church. You see men who once stood for truth now selling their soul for the sake of a large church and prestige among the brethren. What many of these pastors don't take into consideration is what their children and grandchildren will become because of their compromising ways.

My friend, God is just as interested in the methods as He is the result. How you do things matters to God. The methods you choose to get your results is as important to God as the result. To think that God doesn't care about the methods is to ignore the Scriptures. 2 Thessalonians 2:15 says, *"Therefore, brethren, stand fast, and hold the traditions which ye have been taught, whether by word, or our epistle."* The *"traditions"* that were taught were the methods by which the Apostles acquired their results. God further emphasized this truth in 2 Thessalonians 3:6 when He says, *"Now we command you, brethren, in the name of our Lord Jesus Christ, that ye withdraw yourselves from every brother that walketh disorderly, and not after the tradition which he received of us."* God not only wanted the church to follow the methods of the Apostles, but He also said to *"withdraw"* from those who didn't follow those methods.

A result-focused church will eventually compromise. The music you listen to does matter to God. The methods you follow do matter to God. The terminology we use is important to God. Many think that gleaning ideas from the result-focused crowd is fine with God, but it is not. Many are destroying the future of the old paths for their children to walk in all for the sake of getting results. Sadly, the results they seek are often never realized as they become floundering churches and ministries that rarely reach anyone for Christ. Several things need to be considered about the importance of every Christian, pastor, church leader and church not falling into Satan's trap of being result-focused.

1. Children always pay for the actions of their parents.

Numbers 14:18 says, *"The LORD is longsuffering, and of great mercy, forgiving iniquity and transgression, and by no means clearing the guilty, visiting the iniquity of the fathers upon the children unto the third and fourth generation."* The children are often the recipients of their parent's sins. This verse is not saying that children will perform their parent's sins, though they may choose to follow in their footsteps; rather, this verse is teaching that children often suffer for the bad decisions that their parents make.

For instance, the children often suffer for their parents choice to divorce to solve their marital issues. This is just one illustration of parents being results-focused over truth and consequences. If parents truly loved their children, they would consider the consequences of their actions before choosing the immediate gratification of present results.

Likewise, many ministry leaders are choosing the results of immediate growth through compromise without considering the consequence that compromise will have on the second and third generation. You may compromise your standards of holiness, but your children will perceive your inability to stand which results in their total disapproval for the Scriptural way of life.

Pastor, before you start canceling church services, you might consider how it will affect the next generation. Before you accept the fleshly music in your church, you might consider where that music will lead the next generation. You can't compromise truth without hurting the core beliefs of the next generation.

2. You should always consider where the next generation will take your actions.

There is always a tomorrow. What you do in moderation today will be done in excess by the next generation tomorrow. Lowering the dress standards today results in scant dress standards for the next generation tomorrow. Diminishing the importance of church attendance and soul winning today results in no soul winning and missing church altogether by the next generation tomorrow. The next generation always takes your changing of holiness standards as a decree that everything you believe is up for change.

Abraham never thought that Lot would choose Sodom and Gomorrah because of his journeying through the land of Egypt. Naomi never considered that her sons would marry heathen women when they "*sojourned*" in the land of Moab. Likewise, most parents never consider where their children will take their small changes to identify with the world. You can excuse your changes and say that you haven't changed, but your children know that you have changed, and your change, in essence, gives them permission to challenge everything you taught them. If you don't want your children to go the way of the world, you would be wise to continue to stand where you have always stood. If what you did was right in the past, it is still right today even if it is not convenient or popular.

3. Focusing on results is infringing on God's area of responsibility.

1 Corinthians 3:7 says, *"So then neither is he that planteth any thing, neither he that watereth; but God that giveth the increase."* You will notice that God is in charge of the increase. The Christian is not to worry about the increase, but the Christian is to focus on planting, watering and reaping the harvest. It is never the Christian's responsibility to worry about what the increase is going to be; it is their responsibility to get the Gospel out in the manner in which God tells them to do it.

When you measure every action by how many people you get to come, you eventually start trimming your message because you won't want to offend someone. The preacher, pastor, ministry leader and Christian must be careful about focusing on the size of their ministry, because that is not their area. Always remember that God's responsibility is the increase, not yours. If you stay focused on giving out the Gospel to the best of your ability like God tells you to do, it won't bother you when you don't see an increase.

The reason many churches go liberal is because they are more worried about numerical growth than truth. These churches have become result-focused instead of truth and consequence focused. Christian, we don't do what we do to grow the church. We do what we do and in the way we do it to please the LORD. If God chooses to keep a church small as they stand for truth, that is His business. You can't worry that your methods are not building a "big" church. The size of your ministry is not your area of concern; that is God's area.

4. The Christian's sole focus should be on doing right all the time.

As a Christian, your sole focus should be on obeying the LORD. If obeying the LORD doesn't produce a large church or ministry, you have succeeded by doing what you are supposed to do which is to obey the LORD. Don't get me wrong; I am not saying that you should use this as an excuse to be lazy, but I am saying that you should never measure the spirituality or the blessings of God on a ministry by the size of that ministry. The emphasis God puts on the church in the Book of Acts is whether they obeyed the LORD. In fact, God commended the disciples in Antioch because they were *"called Christians."* (Acts 11:26) The results take care of themselves if you will take care of your responsibility to obey the LORD.

5. The future of the old paths is dependent on Christians continuing to use the methods they were taught.

One of the reasons we must never compromise for the sake of results is that the perpetuity of the old paths in our nation is dependent upon every generation walking those paths. Judges 2:10 says, *"…there arose another generation after them, which knew not the LORD, nor yet the works which he had done for Israel."* This generation didn't know the works of the LORD because the previous generation compromised those paths. The next generation's knowledge of the old paths is dependent upon you passing them down to them without compromise. Don't fall into the trap of being result-focused; rather, stay focused on doing right and how that affects tomorrow's consequences and let the LORD determine the results.

Chapter 13

LOWERING THE BAR

When I was a boy, it was not uncommon for preachers to talk about the importance of the youth desiring to surrender to serve the LORD full time. It didn't matter whether you were going to a youth conference or whether you were attending a youth rally, preachers often preached about the importance of young people surrendering to be a preacher, missionary, evangelists, or some type of full-time servant.

Giving the call for full-time service was not something for which we apologized. It was not something that people criticized because it was just one of those things that we expected our young people to do. It was how my generation grew up. It was what our churches used to do back in the days when we set the standard high for the youth to surrender for full-time service.

This resulted in colleges being filled with young people who had a burning desire to go and become a full-time servant for the LORD Jesus Christ. It was not uncommon to see young people surrender in every service to be a preacher, evangelist, Christian schoolteacher, or a missionary. Setting the standard high for young people was common.

Because of the high standard that was set, many young people wanted to become a part of the crowd who served the LORD full-time. Those were the days when churches were being started regularly around the country because we had plenty of young people who were surrendering to full-time service.

When I was a boy, it was not uncommon for my parents to tell me that they wanted me to be a preacher one day. Though they were not the ones who put the call of God on my life, it was their setting the bar high for my life that caused me to look at the possibility of becoming a preacher. At the age of 13, is when I finally surrendered my life to be a preacher of the Gospel of Jesus Christ. I do not regret one moment of my parent's emphasis on full-time service in my life.

Somehow, we have lowered the bar in our churches and homes. We have come to a time in our fundamental Baptist churches when preachers often say that they don't want to have Mama called Papa led young people going into the ministry; as if this is really what has happened. Because of a few pastors who went into the ministry and fell in sin, the Devil has fooled our pastors and youth pastors into believing that we are the ones forcing people to go into the ministry through emotional invitations. Moms and dads, youth departments, and Christian schools have lowered the standard for children to believe that the call of God is some type of emotional moment that only a few will ever experience.

Let me make emphatically state that young people will aim below whatever standard you set for them. I believe that the lowering of the standards in our homes, churches and youth departments to serve the LORD full-time is what has led to a dearth of young people surrendering for full-time service. 1 Timothy 3:1 reminds us, *"This is a true saying, If a man desire the office of a bishop, he desireth a good work."* There is nothing wrong with setting the standard high for our youth to serve the LORD full time so that they will desire to be that preacher or full-time servant of the LORD.

I believe the lowering of the standard is what has led to our young people going to the world because mom and dad, the pastor and youth pastor have all somehow rallied around this notion that it is a bad thing to set the standard high for young people to desire to serve the LORD full time. If we continue to go down this path, there will come a day when there will be a shortage of preachers and full-time servants to fill our pulpits, and that day is coming quickly.

I recently heard how the Southern Baptist churches have a scarcity of young people surrendering to full-time service, so they are recruiting young preachers among our fundamental Baptists churches to fill their pulpits. They are trying to woo our young preachers over to them because they don't have any young people going into the ministry themselves. How did this happen? It happened when they lowered the standard for their youth to serve the LORD full time and made it very clear that they are just happy if their children will just serve the LORD.

If the fundamental Baptists are not careful, we will end up facing the same crisis that the Southern Baptists are experiencing. If we continue to lower the standard for our youth and tell them that our great desire is that they just serve the LORD, we will find ourselves searching for people to fill our empty pulpits.

The Scripture says in Romans 10:14-15, *"How then shall they call on him in whom they have not believed? and how shall they believe in him of whom they have not heard? and how shall they hear without a preacher? And how shall they preach, except they be sent? as it is written, How beautiful are the feet of them that preach the gospel of peace, and bring glad tidings of good things!"*

The problem that we face today is a problem that has come about because we've lowered the standard for the youth. If you ask young people just to serve the LORD, that is the most that they will ever do. However, if you raise the standard high and let them know that your desire is for them to serve the LORD full-time as a preacher, evangelist, missionary, Christian school teacher, pastor's wife, missionary wife, evangelist's wife, or a church secretary, you will continue to see many of these young people surrendering to God's call. It is when we lower the standard that they stop listening for God's call.

I ask you; why is it so bad for young people to surrender to full-time service? Why is it so bad for people to desire to become a full-time servant of the LORD? I often talk to young people who tell me that they are not called to be a preacher. I always respond by asking them, "What has God called you to do?" They often say that they don't know what God has called them to do, but they want to become a businessman or some career of their desire. My response to that young person is this; If God has to call a young man to go into full-time service, God also has to call a young person to be a business person. If God has to call someone to be a missionary, God also has to call a young person to be a police officer. If God has to call someone to be an evangelist, God also has to call a young person to be a lawyer. If God has to call someone to be a full-time servant, God also has to call a young person to be a physician or to do whatever they desire to do because God made us for a specific purpose, and that is to do His will for our lives.

My friend, if we cannot volunteer to become a preacher of the Gospel, we also cannot volunteer to go in the secular world. I believe that we've got to raise the standard once again. I believe that the Book of Romans makes it very clear when Jesus said, *"I beseech you therefore, brethren, by the mercies of God, that ye present your bodies a living sacrifice, holy, acceptable unto God, which is your reasonable service."* (Romans 12:1)

Presenting your body is volunteering to serve the LORD. God does accept volunteers. God does accept young people who will say, "I'll go and do something for the LORD full-time." It always amazes me how we allow young people who are 18 and 19 years old to go and defend our freedoms around the world, but our young people are too young to become pastors, missionaries, evangelists, or full-time servants straight out of Bible College. Let me make this clear; if God can use young people to save our freedoms, God can also use young people to preach the Gospel of Jesus Christ.

Was it not a young teenage boy at 17 years of age who went and defeated Goliath? Why is it that we believe that God is not powerful enough to give young people today the wisdom to serve Him? It's time we set the standard higher. It's time that we stop lowering the standard and cowering to the Devil's attack that we just don't want to force young people into full-time service.

For your information, I've never seen one young person who was forced into full-time service. Those who surrendered went because they chose to do so. Those who surrendered went because they volunteered to go. Was it not Isaiah who said, "...Here am I; send me."? God does accept volunteers! There are several things I would like to bring to your attention about the dangers of lowering the standard and the reason we should raise the standard for youth to serve the LORD full-time.

1. God always sets the standard at the highest level.

Ecclesiastes 9:10 says, *"Whatsoever thy hand findeth to do, do it with thy might..."* Throughout the Scriptures, you will see that God's standard is always excellence. That is why God says in Leviticus 20:26, *"And ye shall be holy unto me: for I the LORD am holy..."* God's command to live for excellence doesn't stop at His call for full-time service. It should be the goal of every church and home that their children live for the highest calling, which is serving the LORD full-time.

2. God's call on one's life is often influenced by adults.

Samuel surrendered to God's call for his life because Eli prepared him for that call. It started when Hannah gave Samuel to serve the LORD full time. Eli followed through with Hannah's commitment for her son by training him and telling him how to listen for the call of God.

Imagine what would happen with our youth if both the parents and the church leaders were on the same page with pointing our youth to serve the LORD full time. Young people will follow the leading of their parents, as they should. If the parents and the church leaders have the mindset to point young people to serve the LORD full-time, there would be no question as to what they should do when the LORD calls.

3. Setting a lower standard always lowers the standard for Christian living.

When you accept the mindset of lowering the bar for the youth, you will eventually lower the bar for the Christian life. I'm always amazed how the churches who don't emphasize to their youth to serve the LORD full-time are also the churches who tend to have a worldly mindset. It truly comes down to what are you trying to do with the children God has given to you? Psalm 127:3 reminds us, *"...children are an heritage of the LORD."* Children are not to be tools to live out our dreams, but they are God's creation to serve Him. When you lower the bar of expectations for your children, they will follow suit and lower the bar of what they deem Christian living.

4. Sinners always choose the path of least resistance.

Sinners never choose the best path of living. Samson ignored God's call and chose the path of least resistance by becoming friends with the enemy. Balaam chose the path of least resistance by ignoring God's call for his life. Whatever the lowest standard is that you set for the youth will be the path they choose to live. The reason you must raise the standard for the youth is so that they will never accept the path of least resistance. You will be surprised how youth will rise to the challenge of God's call if you emphasize its greatness.

5. Point your children to the Scriptures to do the most for Christ.

The Scriptures always lead children to do what God has made them to do. One thing I have pointed out to many people is that God's call is placed on a person at birth. The children of the priests and Levites had no choice but to be priests and servants in the temple because they were born into these families. God knows what family He placed your children in, and if He gave them a godly heritage, they have an obligation to serve the LORD full-time and pass the heritage on to the next generation. The importance of your children reading the Scriptures daily will be seen when they understand God's purpose for their life is to serve Him full-time.

6. Start early in pointing the youth to full-time service.

As I mentioned earlier in this chapter, my parents started preparing my heart at an early age to become a preacher. For those who don't like what I'm saying, why don't you get upset with those parents who train their children at a young age to become sports prodigies? Every parent needs to understand that their purpose is to prepare their children to hear God's call for their life just like Eli trained Samuel to hear God's voice.

7. Get the youth under preaching.

One of the best ways to get your children to surrender for full-time service is to get them under good, Scriptural and passionate preaching. 1 Corinthians 1:18 says, *"For the preaching of the cross is to them that perish foolishness; but unto us which are saved it is the power of God."* Good preaching has a way of challenging young people to serve the LORD with their lives.

8. Keep your youth exposed to full-time servants.

One of the best ways to help youth desire to serve the LORD full time is to get them around full-time servants. My father always allowed me to tag along with him whenever he had guest preachers preaching in our church. The exposure to these preachers created a desire in my heart to become a preacher.

You will do yourself a huge favor by getting your children around full-time servants of the LORD. You will find when you make the pastors, evangelists, missionaries and full-time servants the heroes in your family that your children will grow up desiring to be full-time servants themselves.

My friend, the hope of any nation is for their youth to surrender to serve the LORD full time. If we continue to lower the standard for our children in regards to their Christianity, we will effectively cause our pulpits to be emptied in years to come. Let me encourage you to raise the standard for your children and youth to serve the LORD full time with their lives. There is nothing that gives a greater satisfaction in a parent than to see their children serving the LORD as a full-time servant.

CHAPTER 14

NANNY STATE
THE BATTLE FOR THE MIND OF CHILDREN

It started in 1965, a British politician used the term "nanny state" to describe the overreach of government into the personal lives of its citizens. Sadly, over time, many of the British people accepted the government's overreach into their homes and personal lives. The influence of the British government's nanny state philosophy influenced parents into believing that it was detrimental for their children to be in church on Sunday night; therefore, they left their children at home with a nanny while the parents went to church.

The result of this nanny state mentality led to the godless society that England is today. What many of those parents did not understand was that public education was not more important than their children hearing the Word of God. These parents forgot that the Word of God is the source of all wisdom and knowledge. The demise of England's love for God and the great revivals started when parents accepted the nanny state mentality that children were too young to need church the same way that their parents did.

Sadly the same nanny state mentality has also crept into the United States. What we don't understand is that the Devil's goal has always been to win the mind of the children. His goal is to get the child's mind by influencing them in any way that parents will allow him to do. He knows that if he can influence the mind of a child while they are young that he can control them when they become an adult. Satan has successfully used the nanny state mentality to steal the minds of our children.

Over the years, we have watched different activities influence children to stay out of church. We have watched children's sports leagues play games on church service nights. Sadly, many children are playing baseball, football and soccer when they should be in church. The Boy Scouts plan activities on Sundays and excuse it by saying that they study the Bible while they are out in the woods. Instead of that child sitting in church where they are supposed to be, the public schools have influenced the minds of children in such a way that they no longer teach, but they indoctrinate children in a godless manner teaching them that God is not real, the Word of God is not true, and that a parent's authority over their lives does not trump the importance of "higher education."

Not only has the government and organizations succumbed to the nanny state mentality, but parents have also fallen for the same trap by allowing their children to be raised in daycares instead of by a loving mother who stays home to train her children. Many parents have gotten to the point where they would rather their children be raised by someone else rather than being inconvenienced by fulfilling their responsibility of parenting. All of these things influence the mind of children away from the spiritual influences of their parents and the church.

The Scriptures are very clear in this manner that the parent's job is to train their children. Proverbs 22:6 says,

"Train up a child in the way he should go: and when he is old, he will not depart from it." Many parents look at their children as a bother or inconvenience and look for ways to get their children "out of their hair" so they can enjoy life.

For years, my wife has been in charge of church nurseries. One of the things that she commonly tells me that happens in the nursery is that mothers are quick to get rid of their children just so they can get away from them. Mothers don't want to work in nurseries because they want a "vacation" from their children. They look at their children almost as if they are a bother instead of being a reward from God.

The Scriptures say, *"Lo, children are an heritage of the LORD: and the fruit of the womb is his reward."* (Psalm 127:3) Let me remind you that not only are our children a heritage of the LORD, but they are also the fruit of the womb. In other words, children are God's reward to the parent. If we're not careful, we will become a society that looks at children as a bother; thus, allowing others to teach them to the detriment not only of our homes and churches, but also of our entire society.

Pharaoh understood the importance of influencing children when one of the compromises he offered to Moses was for the parents to go and worship God, but leave their children in the land of Egypt. Sadly, we have found that many parents have accepted Pharaoh's offer to serve the LORD, but have allowed their children to be raised by babysitters, daycares, youth pastors and Christian schools rather than fulfill their responsibility of raising their children.

We must be careful that we as Christians don't become another casualty of the nanny state mentality. I'm finding that many churches are creating programs that keep children away from their parents instead of allowing the children to sit with their parents in church and listen to the preacher. I find that children today don't know how to sit in church or listen because they have never been trained to do so by their parents. There is an epidemic of troubled children mostly because everyone else is training the children instead of the parents fulfilling their responsibility to do so. Let me give you several thoughts on this danger of the nanny state mentality and the responsibility that every parent has in training their children.

1. It is the parent's responsibility to train children.

God always intended for parents to be the main influence on their children. God commanded parents in Proverbs 22:6, "Train up a child in the way he should go: and when he is old, he will not depart from it." It is not the job of the school, youth pastor, babysitter or daycare to train children; it is the parent's responsibility to train their children. Ephesians 6:4 says, "And, ye fathers, provoke not your children to wrath: but bring them up in the nurture and admonition of the Lord." Notice that the parents are the influencers, not an outside person. God commended Abraham when He said about him in Genesis 18:19, "For I know him, that he will command his children and his household after him, and they shall keep the way of the LORD..." It is unscriptural for a parent to pass the training of their children on to anyone else. Your responsibility as a parent is to be the primary influence and trainer in your child's life.

2. Children left to themselves will always bring shame to their parents.

Proverbs 29:15 says, *"The rod and reproof give wisdom: but a child left to himself bringeth his mother to shame."* Leaving a child to themselves is what happens when others begin to be the primary influencers in a child's life. Because the parents are not doing their job, another person normally takes the place of a parent, which leaves confusion in the mind of the child. Therefore, when opinions, knowledge or information differ, the child is left to choose who or what is right. In essence, they are left to themselves, which the Scriptures teach always brings shame to the parents.

3. Training children can't be done through correspondence.

You cannot be a parent who tells your child, "Don't do as I do, but do as I say do." This is the worst type of parenting. Parents are to be the example for their children. Deuteronomy 6:7 says, *"And thou shalt teach them diligently unto thy children, and shalt talk of them when thou sittest in thine house, and when thou walkest by the way, and when thou liest down, and when thou risest up."* Nowhere in this verse does it show that a parent is to train their child from a distance; rather, God makes it clear that training is a hands-on approach that works by directing the children to do right. A correspondence mentality in training children tells the child that what they are told is not that important; thus, they will follow the weaknesses of their parents.

4. Training children must be done by walking in the way with them.

When the Scriptures say, *"Train up a child in the way he should go..."* it means that the parent must be in the way while they are training their child. You can't teach your children how to do right when others are training them. You must be the one to show them how to live. It is the parent's responsibility to show them how to do right and avoid wrong. Every parent will discover that they will be able to win the heart and influence the mind of their child much easier if they are walking in the way with their child.

5. Children need to be in church to hear the preacher.

1 Corinthians 1:21 says, *"For after that in the wisdom of God the world by wisdom knew not God, it pleased God by the foolishness of preaching to save them that believe."* One of the reasons children need to be under the preaching is so that the LORD can do a work in their heart. Children will better learn how to listen to preaching by being in the preaching service with their parents. I'm afraid many churches have good intentions when they offer children's programs that take them out of the services, but most of these programs are entertainment based and not preaching based. Children need to hear preaching just as much as their parents do. Trust me; your children are getting preached to every other day of the week when they sit in school, listen to music, and watch TV. If you don't get them under scriptural preaching, their mind will be influenced by the world's preachers. The battle for the mind can be won much easier if you get your children under the preaching of your pastor.

6. How you train your children will determine the way for the next generation.

The hope of any nation is what the present generation is trained to do. If you adopt the nanny state mentality of allowing others to train your children, you will one day regret that mentality when they grow up and do things you thought they would never do. Many parents live with heartache trying to figure out where their children learned some of the things they do. The answer is that they learned it when their parents stopped walking in the way with them.

The purpose of this chapter is not to sway the parent from allowing other good influences in their children's lives, but it is to stress the importance of taking the responsibility to train them themselves. Satan is after the mind of your children. You must guard your children from any influence that would corrupt their mind, and the only way you will be able to do that is by training them in the way.

CHAPTER 15

I AM A VOICE
THE ATTACK AGAINST PREACHING

John the Baptist said when asked who he was, *"...I am the voice of one crying in the wilderness, Make straight the way of the Lord, as said the prophet Esaias."* John didn't say; I am the voice that goes verse-by-verse preaching the Scriptures; no, He just said, *"I am the voice."* John did not say, I am the one who exegetes the Scriptures, but he said, *"I am the voice."* John did not say that he was a topical voice, he just said, *"I am the voice."* He did not say; I'm the expository voice of the Scriptures; no, he just said, *"I am the voice."* The only thing those people needed was a voice. It didn't matter to John how the voice was delivered; those people just needed John to be the voice for God that cried in the wilderness.

This world is in desperate need of a voice. It doesn't matter if the voice chooses to be topical, the world just needs a voice. It doesn't matter if the voice decides to be expository, the world just needs a voice. It doesn't matter if the voice chooses to go verse-by-verse, the world just needs a voice. It doesn't matter if the voice decides to exegete the Scriptures, the world just needs a voice. You see, this world is in need of a voice that will take the Word of God and deliver it to people because God's Word is what changes lives. People are in need of a voice.

The need for the lost sinner is a voice that will preach the Scriptures. The need of a sinful nation is a voice that preaches the Word of God. The need for revival is going to be accomplished when there is a voice that preaches God's Word. You see it's always a voice that is needed.

Nineveh needed a voice, but they were void of a voice because of a preacher who chose to run. The Nation of Israel needed a voice, but they did not have a voice because preachers chose to preach their own desires and teach their own methods in an attempt to please the people instead of preaching God's Word. It is easy to see that there is a need for a voice.

The book of Romans says, *"How then shall they call on him in whom they have not believed? and how shall they believe in him of whom they have not heard?* **and how shall they hear without a preacher**?" (Romans 10:14) The preacher is the voice that the people need.

Zacchaeus was in need of a voice to show him the way of salvation. Jesus became that voice when He said to Zacchaeus, *"...Zacchaeus, make haste, and come down; for to day I must abide at thy house."* (Luke 19:5) Without Jesus being a voice, Zacchaeus would have gone to Hell.

Nicodemus, the one who came to Jesus by night, was in need of a voice. It didn't matter if the voice was topical, expository, or textual, he just needed to hear a voice to show him how to get saved. Nicodemus just needed to hear, *"Verily, verily, I say unto thee, Except a man be born again, he cannot see the kingdom of God."* (John 3:3) It was the voice he heard that helped him to accept Christ as His Saviour.

Every nation is in need of a voice. The need for Hezekiah was to hear the voice preaching the Word of God. The voice Hezekiah heard was the voice of Isaiah who preached God's Word. It really didn't matter how the voice was delivered to Hezekiah; he just needed to hear a voice. It didn't matter if the voice was topical, textual, or expository, he just needed to hear a voice preach God's Word.

There may be times when the voice may be a lonely voice, but there is a need for a voice. John the Baptist was a voice in the wilderness, but at least his generation had a voice. John fulfilled the need that every nation has, and that is the need of a voice.

We live in times when people are critical of preaching styles. Some say you need to preach topical sermons. Others say expository preaching is the scriptural method of preaching. There are some who mandate that textual preaching is the best. My admonition to every person is that the need is simply a voice. Let me remind you that Jesus was a voice. Just like John the Baptist was a voice for his generation, Jesus was the voice of God to the lost world. He was a voice that taught and preached topical sermons called parables. He was a voice that took the Scriptures and expounded upon them. He was also a voice that quoted the Scriptures verse-by-verse so that those who heard Him couldn't say that they didn't hear the truth.

Simply put, Christians today need to stop worrying about how the voice delivers God's Word and just be glad that you have a voice. Stop worrying if the voice is coming through a megaphone or a microphone; just be a voice. Stop worrying if the voice is topical or expository; just be a voice. You see, the Word of God needs a voice that will be the vehicle to carry it to the ears of a lost world. The Word of God needs a voice that will carry it to the sinner in need of repentance. The world needs a voice that tells the fallen about the grace of Jesus Christ. Every nation needs a voice that will expose their sins so that they will repent and come back to Jesus.

The need of every generation and the need of this day is a voice. The attack against topical preaching is ridiculous because people just need a voice. Whether or not your voice is going to be direct and say we're going to preach on this topic, may I just be honest with you, just be a voice. Let me give you several thoughts concerning the need of a voice.

1. There's always been an attack against preaching.

The attack against topical preaching comes because topical preaching tends to be focused on one topic. You will find that those who attack topical preaching don't like it, not because it is not scriptural, but because it exposes their sins and lifestyle.

The false prophets of Jeremiah's day didn't like his topical preaching because He exposed their sin. The worldly preacher will always criticize the topical preacher because it is pointed preaching. Those prophets attacking Jeremiah was more about what he said than it was about how he said it.

God told Isaiah in Isaiah 58:1, *"Cry aloud, spare not, lift up thy voice like a trumpet, and shew my people their transgression, and the house of Jacob their sins."* How are you going to show people their transgressions and sins if you don't preach topically? One of the greatest ways to be specific about sin is to preach a topical sermon. No, it won't always be the most popular sermon, but those who hear it will know that they have heard the truth.

2. Every sermon should be topical, expository and textual.

If we are honest about preaching, every sermon has a topic; every sermon should be textual and kept in context; and, every sermon should be expository in that it scripturally explains the verses being read. I have always said that the best sermons are the ones that take God's truths and places them on the bottom shelf so everyone can understand them. One of the compliments of Jesus' preaching was that the *"common people heard him gladly."* (Mark 12:37) The common people understood Jesus because He took the Scriptures (textual) and expounded upon them (expository) in a topical manner. Stop fighting over which style a preacher should preach, and realize that a scriptural sermon will have all of these components included in the sermon.

3. A topical sermon is important so you can be precise in fixing the problems.

One of the needs of people is clarity in what the preacher is saying. It was the woman of Samaria who said about Jesus, *"Come, see a man, which told me all things that ever I did: is not this the Christ?"* (John 4:29) Jesus didn't preach in vague terms, but in plain terms which exposed the things this lady had done. If a sermon is going to do what God intends for it to do, it must be topical in nature because it deals directly with man's problems. Let me ask you, how are you going to help the hurting, discouraged, lonely, or a person bound by sin without being topical so you can deal directly with that subject? If every preacher were honest, they all preach topical sermons if they are helping people. In fact, the fact you have a title dictates that you have chosen a topic about which to preach.

4. Expository sermons are important so people learn the Word of God.

When Jesus walked with the two disciples on the road to Emmaus, He helped them by preaching an expository sermon. Luke 24:27 says, *"And beginning at Moses and all the prophets, he expounded unto them in all the scriptures the things concerning himself."* It was Jesus expounding the Scriptures that caused them to say, *"…Did not our heart burn within us, while he talked with us by the way, and while he opened to us the scriptures?"* (Luke 24:32) Just as much as believers need sermons to be topical in nature, they also need to hear the Scriptures expounded upon so that they can understand clearly what they need to do.

5. Textual sermons are important so people keep God's Word in context.

I cannot overemphasize the importance of being textual. Preachers must be careful about twisting a verse to make it fit what they want it to say. When preachers keep their sermons textual, the topic they preach will become clearer and more powerful as they expound the Scriptures.

6. Every style of sermon will help as long as Scripture is proclaimed.

The most important thing we should learn is that every preaching style compounded together will help as long as the Scripture is being proclaimed. 2 Timothy 3:16 says, *"All scripture is given by inspiration of God, and is profitable…"* It doesn't matter if the Scriptures are given in a topical, expository, or textual style; if Scripture is given it is profitable.

7. Stop attacking the messenger's style and be happy that there is a messenger.

I have listened to scores of preachers in my lifetime, and most of the preachers have helped me in my Christian walk. All of these preachers had different styles and delivery, but their sermons touched my heart and helped me to become the believer and preacher I am today. I'm just glad that they were God's messenger to help.

My friend, stop attacking the messenger because he doesn't fit the style of preaching that you like. Instead of attacking the messenger's style, you might ask yourself if his style is offensive because the message he is preaching is convicting. Every believer, and especially every preacher, should be happy that there are messengers who are being a voice for God.

8. When you focus on the preaching style, you miss the truth God has for you.

If you are so focused on the vehicle that the messenger is using to deliver God's truth, you will miss the truth God has for you. There are certain styles of preaching that I am not really fond of, but I am not going to critique the messenger and miss the truth because they are not preaching in my favored style. Every voice who preaches God's Word has a truth that will help if you will just listen and not be concerned with the vehicle they use in delivering that truth.

Let me remind you that the person who is happiest when preaching is attacked is the Devil. Let me encourage you not to do the Devil's work of attacking preaching; instead, be pleased that there is a voice still crying in the wilderness. If we silence the voices that we don't like, we will silence truth; and when truth is silenced, only the lies propagated by Satan's preachers will be heard.

The need of this nation is preaching. If the preaching voice is topical; Amen! If the preaching voice chooses to be an expository voice; Wonderful! If the preaching voice is textual in content; Praise the LORD! Be a cheerleader of the voices proclaiming the truth because as long as there is a voice, there is still hope for every person and nation.

Chapter 16

THE UNDERMINING OF AUTHORITY

One of the ways that liberals have tried to destroy our country is through the undermining of authority. Liberals know very well that the way to destroy a society is by destroying the authorities who are in place. They learned this from the Garden of Eden when Lucifer tried to destroy God's authority over Adam and Eve. Just like Lucifer, liberals try to undermine authority by questioning them. Once liberals get you to question authority, they then attempt to make you feel that you need to become your own authority, which is exactly what Lucifer did when he told Eve that she would become *"as gods, knowing good and evil."* (Genesis 3:5) Once you accept the premise that you are your own authority, you have then replaced God by accepting the wrong authority.

This is one of the ways that the left is destroying our society. They know that they can create internal chaos and overthrow our democracy if they can get every citizen to question authority. The liberals started undermining authorities years ago when they printed bumper stickers that said, "Question Authority." They were not trying to get you to verify by God's Word an authority's actions or words, but they wanted you to question every decision made by authority. It is an age-old problem where people are always challenging authority, and the reason they challenge authority is because they think that they are always right and that authority is always wrong. Today's authority is constantly under attack, and we see the result of this destruction through the chaotic actions of people in our country.

The Devil knows that he can do the same thing in our churches and homes if he can undermine the authority of these institutions as well. If he is successful in undermining the authority in the home and church, he knows that homes will be broken and churches will be destroyed. We must always guard against the Devil's attempt to undermine authority.

What I have found is that many times the undermining of authority often comes through authorities. When I look at the God-given roles of authority, I always realize that the highest authority is God. We must never forget that God is the highest authority. When we forget that God is the highest authority is when Satan moves in and gets people to make themselves their own authority, which results in personal chaos in the lives of those whom that authority affects.

Sadly, many times pastors reach beyond their authority and hurt the homes that are a part of their church. Let me remind every pastor that the authority of the home after God are the parents. No pastor or youth pastor should ever question the parent's right to parent their children by outwardly disagreeing with them over their decisions for their children. The parents are responsible for those children, not that pastor or youth pastor. When a parent tells their teenager that they can't go to a youth activity, the youth pastor should never get that teenager to question their parent's decision. Instead, that youth pastor should support the parent's decision of not sending their children to the activity. If that youth pastor has a problem, he needs to go to the parents and respectfully ask if there is a problem that they can help with instead of demanding that the parents support the church program.

My friend, the purpose of the church program is to support the family. Yes, the family should be involved in the church, but the purpose of the church's program is to help build the family. God started the church to help people, and we must never use people to build the church, but we must always use the church to build people.

Likewise, a pastor must be careful about intervening in a marriage and overstepping his bounds. The head of that marriage is the husband, and when a pastor steps in and begins to rebuke the wife, that pastor has overstepped his authority. It is the husband's job to make sure that his wife follows the LORD. If the pastor has a problem with a lady in the church, he needs to go to the husband and ask for his help. A pastor should always be respectful of the husband's authority in the marriage and home.

Pastors, let me warn you about becoming accusative of a man's wife. If you become accusative of a man's wife and undermine his authority by overstepping your authority, you will soon lose the trust of that couple and probably their membership. The pastor's job is to help the family from the pulpit, and support the roles of authority in the marriage and home.

Likewise, church members must be careful about overstepping the roles of the pastor in the church. It is just as wrong for a person to tell the pastor how to run the church as it is for the pastor to overstep his authority and try to run the homes. The pastor is the one responsible to God for that church, and any church member who gossips and tries to undermine the role of that pastor is disobeying God's divine role for the authority in the church. When a person undermines the authority of the church, they will lose their authority with their children and with those whom they lead. You must be careful that you don't undermine authorities.

Let me emphatically say that the pastor should cheer the parents as the parents rear their children. The parents should cheer the authorities of the school, but the school must never overstep its boundaries and tell the parents what to do with their children. That child belongs to the parent, and not to the government or the school. The child is not a property of the state, but a reward of God to the parent. Likewise, we must support each other when it comes to the church and not undermine that authority because undermining the authority in a church will cause hurt to that church.

There are several things we must always keep in mind about authority so that we don't undermine it and destroy the very things that we love. If we love our children, we will make sure that we follow these observations concerning authority. If a pastor or a church leader truly loves the people whom they are serving; they will be sure to support the roles of authority and not undermine them or overstep their lines of authority. Let me give you several thoughts concerning the importance of staying in the role of authority so that we don't fall into Satan's trap of undermining authority.

1. **There is more than one authority to which you will have to submit.**

   Romans 13:1 says, *"Let every soul be subject unto the higher powers. For there is no power but of God: the powers that be are ordained of God."* You will notice that God says, *"higher powers."* The word *"powers"* shows that there is always going to be more than one power or authority in your life. For instance, a child's authorities may consist of God, parents, pastor, teachers, or any adult their parents place them under. An adult's authorities may consist of God, spouse, pastor, boss, civil servants, or any form of leadership they choose to serve under. These are just two areas of illustration, but you must understand that there is always going to be more than one authority in your life.

2. **Each authority must understand the reach of their power.**

   God says that every soul is to be *"subject unto the higher powers."* In other words, you may be an authority in one area, but you may not be an authority in another area. For instance, a pastor is the authority of the church, but not the authority in another's home. The parent is the authority in their home, but they are not the authority in the church. The policeman is the authority as they patrol the streets of their city, but they are not the authority of a church or someone else's home. Likewise, a business owner is the authority of the business they own, but they are not the authority to tell the pastor how to run the church. Just because you are an authority in one area doesn't give you the right to tell another authority how to run their area when it is not your area of authority. All authorities must understand the limits of their power and be careful about reaching into areas of power which do not belong to them.

3. No authority is to reach into another's area of authority.

One of the biggest problems that cause confusion is when one authority reaches into another's area of authority. For instance, a child is taught to listen to authority, but when one authority tries to tell a child what to do when the parent's have already told them what to do, that child is brought to the point of confusion of not knowing whom to obey.

Likewise, one pastor doesn't have the right to tell another pastor how to run their church. Each pastor's power of authority only belongs to their local church. This principle could be applied to civic leaders, leaders of nations, and business owners. It is never right for one authority to tell another authority what they are supposed to do when it is not their area of authority.

4. Authorities will not always agree.

I know this is going to shock you, but every authority will not agree with each other. The danger of being an authority is that most authorities have strong opinions on how they think things should be run. Often, those authorities will voice their areas of disagreement, which is not helpful to building productive lives. Authorities are going to disagree at times, but you must not allow yourself to get involved in their disagreements because you will always find yourself having to apologize for your wrong.

5. When authorities disagree, you should always submit to the highest authority.

Notice Romans 13:1 says, *"Let every soul be subject unto the higher powers."* The emphasis is on the *"higher powers."* Whenever authorities disagree in your life, always obey the higher authority. For instance, God is **ALWAYS** the higher authority. If any authority wants you to disobey God, always obey God because He is the higher authority.

However, there are times when you are faced with authorities under God who disagree. For instance, the parent is a higher authority for a child than the school. A school should never make a child have to decide whether to obey their parents or their teacher. When a child is faced with this decision, they should always obey their parents because they are the higher authority.

When you have to choose whether to obey a supervisor or a plant manager, you always obey the plant manager for they are the higher power. When a church ministry disagrees with the parent, the child is always to obey their parent for they are the higher power. When a pastor wants a Christian to do something that is against God, they should always obey God. For instance, if a pastor tells a church member to lie, they should obey God and tell the truth. Never do wrong for the authority when God's Word is clear on the matter.

Whenever you are faced with two authorities who disagree on what you should do, always determine who is the highest authority in that area, then obey the higher power. You will always be safe by placing yourself under the higher power.

THE UNDERMINING OF AUTHORITY

6. Improper roles of authority contribute to confusion.

God says in 1 Corinthians 14:33, *"For God is not the author of confusion, but of peace, as in all churches of the saints."* Satan is always trying to cause confusion in our lives to distract the believer away from God's absolutes. One of the greatest reasons the church of Corinth was so filled with confusion and gross sin was because they allowed the wrong people to fill the positions of authorities. They had ladies usurping the authority of men, which led to confusion.

Confusion always occurs any time a leader steps out of their area of authority to undermine the true authority. If you don't want to contribute to a person's confusion on what the LORD wants them to do, you are going to have to stay in your area of authority. Undermining another authority because you don't like them or disagree with them is never going to help the cause of Christ; instead, it always leads to confusion.

7. Improper use of an authority's power leads to hurt.

1 Peter 5:2-3 says, *"Feed the flock of God which is among you, taking the oversight thereof, **not by constraint**, but willingly; not for filthy lucre, but of a ready mind; Neither as being lords over God's heritage, but being ensamples to the flock."* Many leaders have hurt people because they lorded over them instead of leading them by example. Any leader who uses intimidation to lead always hurts those whom they lead. The greatest leader won't have to intimidate people to follow them because their example will motivate people to want to follow.

8. Supporting your authority authenticates your authority.

You show others how to follow you when you choose to follow your authority. Every leader is teaching their follower when they choose to support the leaders in each area. When a follower sees another leader submitting to their leader, they validate the importance of submitting to authority. If you want others to follow you in your area of authority, you would be wise to submit to other authorities when you are in their area.

9. Destroying your authority causes others to question your authority.

You can talk bad about other authorities, but you must remember that your followers are learning from your lead. If you criticize other leaders, you can expect your followers to criticize you. The best way to keep your followers from questioning your decisions is not to question the decisions of authorities in your life.

10. When authorities are wrong, they must admit their wrong.

Let me emphatically say; authority is not always right. I know this isn't what we have heard throughout the years, but no authority is always right because every authority is a sinner. The wisest thing an authority can do when they are wrong is to admit their wrong. Your followers know when you are wrong, and you will gain their respect and trust when you learn to admit and apologize when you have done wrong.

THE UNDERMINING OF AUTHORITY

11. Give authority a break; they are human.

Finally, every follower has to remember that their authority is human, and a human is at times going to do wrong. Let me warn you about always criticizing the authority when they do wrong. Give authority a chance to make a mistake without destroying them. Certainly, if an authority is constantly making mistakes something has to be done, but never fall into the trap of expecting every leader to be perfect and without error. When an authority makes a mistake, pray for them to be better the next time instead of criticizing them.

Satan is out to destroy every authority. His goal is to undermine authorities so that he can create chaos in our lives. Don't be a part of his agenda. Always remember that God is great enough to take care of wrong authorities. Make it your habit to support the higher authority in your life. Also, be sure if you are an authority that you stay in your area of authority so that you don't become a tool of Satan to undermine authority.

CHAPTER 17

THE CHURCH REDEFINED

Satan always offers substitutes for anything that God has established. When God established marriage, Satan offered adultery. When God offered good music, Satan offered rock music. When God offered truth, Satan offered lies. Satan always has a substitute for everything that God has given us in His Word. Whenever you see something that God has given in His Word, you will always find Satan's substitute is not that far behind, and his substitute always seems more appealing to the flesh than to the Spirit.

This has truly happened with the local New Testament Baptist Church. We find that Satan has hated the church since Christ started it in Mathew, and he has offered many substitutes for the church. When you look in the New Testament, you will see that the synagogue was a substitute for those who preached the Gospel of Jesus Christ. Because the people of Christ's day didn't want to be part of the local New Testament Baptist church, they joined their local synagogue which promoted the law over Jesus' sacrificial death for their sins. You see, Satan always has a substitute for anything that God has established.

We live in times when modern churches have strayed from what they once used to believe. I look across our nation and see men and churches who once used to trumpet truth and now have become worldly. These churches are destroying the foundations of a scriptural church. The Scriptures say in Psalm

11:3, *"If the foundations be destroyed, what can the righteous do?"* Satan is doing his best to destroy the foundations of the old paths through these modern fleshly churches that are very appealing to the flesh.

The attack by the world against the church is no surprise. Hollywood has attacked the church; government has attacked the church, and yet the church still stands. Why? Because Jesus promised, *"...the gates of hell shall not prevail against it."* (Matthew 16:18) It doesn't matter what Satan throws at the local New Testament Baptist church; the church is always going to stand.

However, we have those from within who are trying to destroy what God has established in the old paths, Baptist church. We are warned of this in Jude 1:3 when God says to *"earnestly contend for the faith which was once delivered unto the saints."* It is interesting that in the book of Jude, God warns the believer to contend for the faith. He then goes further to warn in verse 4, *"For there are certain men crept in unawares, who were before of old ordained to this condemnation, ungodly men, turning the grace of our God into lasciviousness, and denying the only Lord God, and our Lord Jesus Christ."*

There is a movement among the fundamental Baptist churches that is using grace as a license for worldliness. They say that because we live in the day of grace, the believer can do whatever they want without worrying of God's judgment because, they say, judgment was finished at Calvary. Though sin's judgment was finished at Calvary, it still doesn't take away the consequences of sin.

This is exactly what the word *"lasciviousness"* is talking about in verse 4. *"Lasciviousness"* means: playful, undesigned, or frolicsome. In other words, God is saying that these men who have crept into the church use grace to create a playful, undesigned church with no loyalty to truth or desire for holiness.

Let me emphatically say to everyone reading this book; grace is not an excuse for the believer to sin. Grace is given to us because we broke God's law; therefore, God's grace enables us to have another chance to serve Him if we live a holy life. Sadly, we have those who have turned the grace of God into a license for the believer to do what they want to do which has resulted in the church looking more like the world than a called out assembly.

This should not surprise us when we look at the identifiers that God gives of those who turn grace into lasciviousness. God gives several identifiers in the book of Jude which properly exposes those who have frustrated the grace of God through their lascivious lifestyle. Let me show you these identifiers.

1. They pattern their church to appeal to the flesh.

Verse 8 says, *"...these filthy dreamers defile the flesh."* Isn't it interesting that many of these churches pattern their programs to make the flesh feel good? They have rock concerts and dramas to draw people in. They drop their Christ-honoring standards of holiness to appeal to the lust of the eyes. They condone men having long hair as long as they sing "Gospel" songs that appeal to the flesh. Why do they do these things? Because they have patterned their ministries to appeal to the flesh.

2. They dislike authority.

Verse 8 continues to say that these *"despise dominion."* In other words, they don't like scriptural authority. It is very interesting that these fleshly churches attack every authority that upholds truth. They often say that they don't believe a man should tell us what to do. To some degree, they sound right, but God designed authority as the tool to deliver His truths. To think that a church should have no authority is directly opposed to the teaching of God's Word.

3. They don't believe in absolute truth.

Notice that verse 8 continues to say, *"…despise dominion, and speak evil of dignities."* There are those in this worldly movement who decry the past leaders of the independent, fundamental Baptist movement. They hate Jack Hyles, Lee Robertson, J. Frank Norris, or any other strong leader from the past who strongly stood for truth. They criticize these men from the past in an attempt to delegitimize the old paths that we are to walk.

4. They don't believe in absolute truth.

Verse 11 says that these people *"ran greedily after the error of Balaam for reward."* This is talking about Balaam not believing in an unchanging, absolute truth. What you will always find about these worldly churches is that they don't believe there is absolute truth. This is why they don't believe that the King James Bible is the inspired and preserved Word of God. You will find on these church's websites that they won't identify what Bible they believe; they just say they believe in the inerrancy of the Scriptures. That's okay to say, but please tell us if you believe the King James Bible is the inspired and preserved Word of God. Don't tell me you believe in the King James Bible when you're not even willing to put it on your church website.

5. They don't believe in structure.

Verse 12 tells that these worldly churches are *"clouds they are without water, carried about of winds."* This is showing that these churches don't believe in scriptural structure. These worldly churches want no structure because they want to be their own authority. That's why they take the name Baptist off their church signs. That is why they want to say they are not going to identify with any group. The reason they don't want to identify with any group is because they hate structure. Again we were warned of this in the book of Jude.

6. These worldly churches place an emphasis on socially accepted terminology.

Verse 16 says about these churches that they will speak *"great swelling words, having men's persons in admiration because of advantage."* The reason they put an influence on socially accepted terminology is because they want to be accepted by society. They no longer use visitation cards; rather, they use connection cards. They no longer have Sunday School; instead, they have circles. They change terminology to be more identified with the world than the church. You see, they want society's approval just like Peter when he denied Christ and began to curse and swear. Though these people don't swear; they are sure to use terminology that isn't "offensive" and more "inclusive" so that they can coax the world to come to their church.

7. They mock those who hold to the faith of the old paths.

Verse 18 says, *"...there should be mockers in the last time, who should walk after their own ungodly lusts."* These who walk these unproven new paths will mock and criticize how the old-time believer serves the LORD. You will find these worldly churches mock what we teach regarding the scriptural way to dress. They criticize men of God who stand for the old paths instead of using Scripture to defend their worldly ways.

8. They place an importance on a conjured spirit instead of the Holy Spirit.

You will notice in verse 19 that it says, *"These be they who separate themselves, sensual, having not the Spirit."* They influence people with their music, and that is what they call their spirit. You will find that the music of these churches appeals to the flesh. Music is a great identifier of the direction of a church. You will always find that those who have left the old paths always go to a worldly music sound to appease the flesh so they can conjure up a spirit in their services, but you can be assured that they will not have the presence of the Holy Spirit.

9. They place great importance on social activism.

Verse 20 says, *"...building up yourselves on your most holy faith, praying in the Holy Ghost,"* Isn't it interesting that God wanted the faith to be what the church was known for and not their social activism. My friend, Jesus didn't go about picking up trash along the highway. Jesus didn't get involved in the social activities of the city. No; Jesus spread the Gospel through personal soul winning. These worldly churches are more interested in being liked by society than being approved by God. Let me conclude by giving you several statements.

1. Truth is absolute

Hebrews 13:8 says, *"Jesus Christ the same yesterday, and to day, and for ever."* Truth never changes. There are many who say that truth is defined by culture or one's conscience, but they are wrong. Truth never changes!

2. God's Word is the final authority.

John 17:17 says, *"Sanctify them through thy truth: thy word is truth."* God's Word is truth, and truth cannot change; therefore, God's Word is the final and only authority. It does not matter what one's conscience says or what culture dictates; it only matters what God's Word commands. You must measure everything you do by God's Word.

3. God believes in structure.

God is a God of structure. When you look in the Old Testament and see how God gave the structure for the temple and sacrifices to Moses, you see that God was setting a pattern for the need of the New Testament church to be structured. When you go to the book of Corinthians and the Epistles of Paul, you will see that there is structure for the

New Testament church. God shows the structure by giving the church a pastor, deacons, teachers and evangelists. God believes in structure, and those who don't want structure are only going against the pattern that is taught in the Word of God.

4. The church should never change.

1 Timothy 3:15 says that the church is *"the pillar and ground of the truth."* If the church is the pillar and ground of truth, that means the church is never to change. Churches today are to use the same methods that the churches of old used. If the bus ministry was used to bring people to church in the past, we then ought to keep running the buses today. If it was right to go soul winning in the past, it is still right to be a soul winner today. If preaching God's Word with authority and power is what Jesus did, we must keep on preaching the Word of God with power and authority.

Let me make it clear, if old-fashioned music is what we are supposed to sing, then we need to continue singing the old hymns of the faith. Why? Because these are the old paths that the church gave to us to follow. It doesn't matter whether or not the methods work; we are to do them because God commands us to do them.

5. Stop looking for new ways.

Jeremiah 6:16 says *"…Stand ye in the ways, and see, and ask for the old paths, where is the good way, and walk therein, and ye shall find rest for your souls…"* Let me challenge you to keep walking the old paths. Stop looking at the worldly churches for ideas and just keep doing what you are supposed to do. If what we do does not work, we are to still do it because it's the right thing to do. Truth never changes because it "doesn't work" in our present day. God never said that we are to do these things so we could build a church, but we are to do them because it is right. God is the One who gives the increase, and if doing right does not bring increase, that should not bother us because that is God's area.

What should bother us is when we start changing to draw a crowd. Let me warn you to be careful of these worldly churches and their substitutes that the Devil has provided. Remember that he always provides substitutes because he knows that the worldly church will destroy the next two generations because they will never teach the whole truth. The only thing these generations will know is the fleshly activities of the world, and they will soon go to the world.

Mark my word; watch the next two generations of these churches that are going the way of the world, and you will see that their children and grandchildren will become people who won't even be in church because they were never taught truth. My friend, stick to the old paths; they always work.

Chapter 18

GROOMING FOR THE WORLD

Several years ago when I was a young boy, the newest candy craze was candy cigarettes. I remember watching all of my friends carry a pack of candy cigarettes around and acting like they were smoking cigarettes. All the boys my age thought it was cool to pretend that they were smoking cigarettes.

One day, I remember going to my mother and asking her if she could buy me candy cigarettes like all my friends. My mother abruptly and sternly answered, "NO!" I looked at my mother as any young boy would do in wonder and asked, "But mom, why can't I have them. They're not real; they're just candy." My mother didn't hesitate at all with her answer as she replied, "Son, we don't play sin in our house."

I didn't quite understand her mentality at the moment, but I now understand my mother's response for a couple of reasons. The first reason was because she didn't ever want someone to mistake her son as one of those boys who actually smoked cigarettes. The second reason was because she didn't want me to get used to having something that looked like a cigarette hanging from my mouth. She wanted me to not only live like a Christian, but she wanted me to look like one too.

Just like the candy cigarette fad, it seems that the latest fad going through our independent Baptist churches is the colored lights on the platform. Many churches are darkening the auditorium lights and replacing the platform lights with colored lights. My fear is that we are desensitizing our youth from sinful atmospheres and grooming them for the world. I know, the leftist independent Baptists are rolling their eyes right now and complaining that I am just nitpicking, but I'm not. There are scriptural reasons as to why we should keep bright lighting in our church auditoriums.

1. The Scriptures command to abstain from all appearances of evil.

Several months ago, a young man visited our college to see if it were the place he would attend. He previously attended another college, but in his words, they were changing. As we sat and talked to each other, my pastor and I asked him if he had any hesitations about attending our college. He said he had one, and that was he didn't know if he liked how strict we were with our music. We replied by asking him to tell us some of his favorite singers and songs to which he enjoyed listening. He told us a title of a song, to which my pastor began searching on the internet for the singer who made that song popular. When we brought up a picture of that singer singing one of his favorite songs, we showed it to him without him knowing who it was and asked him if he knew who was singing and the place where he was performing. He thought it was either a rock concert or a bar setting. We then told him that this was his favorite singer singing in a so-called Baptist church. He was totally astonished, not because of the music, but because of the appearance.

1 Thessalonians 5:22 says, *"Abstain from all appearance of evil."* Our churches have no business looking like rock

concerts or bar scenes. It is sad that most people who came out of the world see the liberal preacher trying to attract people by looking more like the concerts and bar scenes than they are with looking like an independent Baptist church. God didn't say abstain from some appearances of evil, but *"all appearance of evil."* Nobody should ever mistake the lighting of our church service for a bar scene or rock concert; instead, people should be able to look at pictures of our services and know it is a church auditorium.

2. It desensitizes the youth to the wrong atmosphere.

Just like my mother didn't want me to get used to sin by playing it, our churches shouldn't desensitize our youth to the atmosphere of sin. Your atmosphere does make a difference. Our youth should never be exposed to sin's atmosphere.

I think of Lot who was desensitized to sin when Abram took him to Egypt. Genesis 13:1 says, *"And Abram went up out of Egypt, he, and his wife, and all that he had, and Lot with him, into the south."* Lot saw the atmosphere of sin, but he never experienced its heartache. The reason Lot chose the plains of Sodom is because he got desensitized to sin when they were in Egypt.

My friend, if you don't want your youth getting used to the world's atmosphere, don't let that atmosphere into your home or church. The dark lighting is Satan's atmosphere. Jesus said in John 3:19 says, *"And this is the condemnation, that light is come into the world, and men loved darkness rather than light, because their deeds were evil."* Only those who love sin love the dimly lit atmosphere where sin is committed.

3. God's children are to be children of light.

Ephesians 5:8 says, *"For ye were sometimes darkness, but now are ye light in the Lord:* **walk as children of light***:"* Notice, before we got saved we were in darkness, but when a Christian gets saved they are to *"walk as children of light."* Paul reminds us in 1 Thessalonians 5:5, *"Ye are all the children of light, and the children of the day: we are not of the night, nor of darkness."*

Church auditorium lighting should represent who we are, *"children of light."* There should be no mistake when people walk into our auditoriums about who we represent because our lighting tells them we are not of the world but are *"children of light."* If for any reason the dark-colored lighting in our auditoriums is wrong, it is because it misrepresents Who we represent.

4. We are to come out of the world, not bring the world into the church.

2 Corinthians 6:17 says, *"Wherefore come out from among them, and be ye separate, saith the Lord, and touch not the unclean thing; and I will receive you,"* Why are churches looking to the world for their ideas when they are supposed to come out of the world? We are not to bring the world's atmosphere, actions, philosophies or form of religion into our churches; instead, we are to be sure that we worship the LORD in the manner by which He designed in His Word. Even

if the Scriptures had not called us *"children of light,"* it would be wrong to copy the world because the church was to come out of the world. My friend, God's church is to be different from the world by God's design. Stop looking to the world for ideas, and start looking to the Scriptures for God's design and pattern.

5. While many may think this is petty, our youth are being groomed to the world's atmosphere.

While many may criticize this chapter, what they don't realize is that their children are being groomed for the world by their religious leaders who have adopted the atmosphere of the world. We should say as Moses said in Exodus 10:9, *"…We will go with our young and with our old, with our sons and with our daughters, with our flocks and with our herds will we go; for we must hold a feast unto the LORD."* Our children need to see the right way to serve the LORD. Certainly, the preachers of Pharaoh will scoff at this article and say that lighting doesn't matter, but it is hard to argue against the fact that we are *"children of light."* Let's stop creating an atmosphere that grooms children to go to the world, and let's create an atmosphere that keeps our children serving the LORD and represents who God saved us to be.

Chapter 19

DON'T MOVE THE PULPIT

Satan's attack against what we believe is methodical and purposeful. He knows that the believer would never accept where he truly wants to take them, so he always makes subtle moves to get the believer to change. It is the character of Satan to be subtle. Genesis 3:1 says, *"Now the serpent was more subtil than any beast of the field which the LORD God had made..."* This serpent was being used by Satan to deceive Eve. In fact, we see that Satan is a serpent in Revelation 20:2 where it says, *"And he laid hold on the dragon, that old serpent, which is the Devil, and Satan, and bound him a thousand years,"* If the serpent in the Garden of Eden was subtle in its moves, so Satan is very subtle in how he gets the believer to change from who they are supposed to be.

One of the areas where Satan is subtly attacking the preaching and identity of the church is by removing the pulpit from the church. There is a movement today to remove the pulpit from the church because they believe it is out-of-date. Satan truly understands the importance of the pulpit getting people to respond to the Word of God, and if he can get the pulpit removed, he will eventually get God's people to remove God's Word from their lives.

Satan's attempt to remove the pulpit started years ago. Again, let me remind you that Satan moves subtly and slowly. For many years, churches never moved the pulpit for anything. Any Christmas play that was to be put on had to plan its decorations around the pulpit. There came a point when some innocently thought it would be good if the pulpit could be removed from the platform so that it wouldn't "interfere" with the Christmas play or cantata. Once the Christmas play was over, men replaced the pulpit back in its place for the pastor to preach.

Once God's people got used to the pulpit being removed for different events the church sponsored, it became common for some preachers to leave the pulpit out because it was too hard to replace it for the preaching time. Again, Satan was doing his part to change the believer's mindset concerning the importance of preaching. It was subtle moves like these that got God's people comfortable with no pulpit on the platform.

Today, many younger preachers are criticizing the use of the pulpit and are saying that we will never reach this present world if we are not willing to remove the pulpit from our platform. There are many younger preachers who have replaced the pulpit with a table where two or three men sit to have a roundtable discussion instead of preaching. These so-called preachers have fallen for Satan's subtle moves to remove God's Word from the church. You can criticize what I am saying, but look at how many of the pulpitless churches are using music to appease the crowd rather than preaching to change the lives of the believer. Look at how these pulpitless churches are more worldly in action and dress. The removing of the pulpit is Satan's subtle move to remove preaching and God's Word from the believer's life. There are several observations I would like to give you about the pulpit and its importance to God's purpose in your life and in the church's influence on people.

1. The pulpit is scriptural.

The first mention of a pulpit is found in Nehemiah 8:4 where it says, *"And Ezra the scribe stood upon a pulpit of wood, which they had made for the purpose…"* What was the purpose for which this pulpit was made? It was made so that Ezra could read God's Word distinctly and give sense to what it said. This is nothing more than the preaching of the Word of God.

The pulpit is not a man-made idea just to have a place for God's Word to be placed, but it is a scriptural principle. The reason we use a pulpit today in our churches is because God showed us the importance of the pulpit through the preaching of Ezra. If God didn't think the pulpit was important to what happened on the day that Ezra read the Scriptures to His people, He would have never mentioned it in the Book of Nehemiah.

2. The pulpit shows the importance of preaching.

It was from the pulpit where Ezra gave sense to God's Word so that the people could understand. By having a pulpit, the church is showing that the primary focus of the church service is the preaching of the Word of God. Why would a church make preaching the central focus? Because preaching is what changes lives. 1 Corinthians 1:18 says, *"For the preaching of the cross is to them that perish foolishness;*

but unto us which are saved it is the power of God." God continues to show the importance of preaching in 1 Corinthians 1:21 where He says, "...it pleased God by the foolishness of preaching to save them that believe."

When you make the pulpit the focal point of the auditorium, you are showing that preaching is the primary purpose of the church service. By removing the pulpit, you are telling those attending that preaching is not important to their lives.

3. The pulpit brings a unified focus.

Nehemiah 8:5 says, "And Ezra opened the book in the sight of all the people..." The reason the pulpit is placed in the center front of the auditorium is because you are pointing the people to look towards one place. God is a God of order. 1 Corinthians 14:40 shows us this when it says, "Let all things be done decently and in order." A preacher knows that it is easier to keep people focused on the preaching of God's Word when they keep the pulpit front and center. Satan already tries to distract the believer from the preaching of the Word of God with so many distractions, so why would you help him by removing the pulpit and creating a divided focus?

4. The pulpit shows the importance of authority.

Nehemiah 8:5 continues to say, "And Ezra opened the book in the sight of all the people; (for he was above all the people;)..." You will notice that not only was there a pulpit, but the pulpit was placed on a platform to allow Ezra to be above the people. The reason he was above the people was because he was the authority God used to deliver His Word to the people.

The pulpit is a place of authority. Whoever stands behind the pulpit holds a grave responsibility to preach God's Word as God intends for it to be preached. Not just anybody should be able to stand behind the pulpit, but only those authorities whom God has ordained to deliver His Word.

One of the main reasons the pulpit is higher than the crowd is to show them the importance of God and His Word. The preacher is God's representative to the people. No, he is not sinless, but he is the one ordained by God to deliver His holy Word. By putting the pulpit higher than the people, you are telling the people that the preaching of God's Word should be something revered and sacred.

5. The pulpit identifies your church to the world.

Everything we do in the church identifies who we are. Let me ask you, how will the world identify what you are if your platform looks more like a stage for a rock concert than it does a platform with a pulpit for the preaching of God's Word? That pulpit does identify you to everyone who visits. Every person knows that a pulpit is a place for preaching.

6. Even the world understands the importance of a pulpit.

Finally, the world has more sense than many of these worldly preachers. When the President gives a speech, he always does so behind a pulpit of wood. The pulpit of wood which the President uses shows his authority and the respect those listening should give. If the world knows the importance of a pulpit, why do God's people fight against its importance?

Satan is very subtle in his attack against the preaching of God's Word. Let me caution you not to fall into his trap of thinking the pulpit is not important. If you remove the pulpit, you can be assured it won't be long before the worldly rock music moves into the services. My friend, leave the pulpit alone. Don't move the pulpit! The pulpit is scriptural, and the removing of it shows a person's disdain for what God established in the Scriptures.

CHAPTER 20

DRESSING DOWN DECENCY

Before the 1950s, men used to dress up to go to ballgames. Anytime you look at pictures of professional ballgames in the 1940s to the early 1950s; you see ladies dressed as if they were going to church and men wearing suits. It was just an expected thing in those days.

Something happened in the 1950s that changed the way society dressed as a whole. James Dean came on the scene with his popular movie, "Rebel Without a Cause." The youth embraced his unbuttoned shirt with blue jeans, as he dressed the part of a rebel. Sadly, his clothing style has become the accepted dress today, but it came about from the mindset of rebelling against the culture that it was proper for men to wear suits and ladies to wear dresses that made this wrong.

In the 1960s, business casual took the place of suits. As the Rock and Roll culture continued its onslaught of rebellion, the dress standards continued to be challenged. The business casual soon changed in the 1970s when the hippie generation took hold in America. Where business casual was once the standard dress, it quickly became the style of the rebel to wear blue jeans as they smoked their dope.

When you look at how society used to dress back in the 40s and 50s, it is with amazement that we look at the sloppy dress of our current culture. The scantly dressed women of today is considered acceptable attire. The men, no longer wear business casual, and instead wear blue jeans and t-shirts, and this is the accepted norm.

Every week when I fly to meetings, I am the abnormality on the airplane as I still travel in my suit and tie. It is sad that how I dress to travel is so different from the normal passenger, and nearly every week brings a comment about my "sharp attire." I don't think I dress sharper than most who wear a suit and tie; it is just so abnormal that those who compliment me are amazed that someone still dresses up to fly.

Dressing down is a mindset and a direction. When you consider how America used to dress compared to how we dress today, you would think there would be no argument against the importance of proper dressing. Who would have ever thought that the ballparks of the 1940s would today be filled with people who reveal nearly everything, leaving the mind with little to nothing to wonder about. When America chose to start dressing down, it led to a mindset and a direction to where decency is no longer expected. Sadly, there are many people today who don't see indecency as indecent; instead, they believe it is just a person expressing themselves and a normal societal way to dress. The indecency seen today as you walk down the streets and in the malls are a direct result of the initial decision to dress down in the 1950s.

Unfortunately, churches have accepted the same mindset and don't realize the direction it is leading. When I was a boy, every parent made their boys wear a suit and tie to church. The only people who didn't wear suits and ties were visitors; however, even many visitors had the common courtesy to dress up for church. As time has passed, parents allowed their boys to wear polo shirts to church to the point that a young man who wears a polo shirt and dress slacks is considered a sharp dresser.

Many churches today look more like a social club instead of a church. I'm amazed at how many preachers excuse casual dress to appease their loosening standards. Though many of these who accept casual wear would say they have not changed; they have changed as they used to understand the importance of dressing up to represent the LORD. Where we used to wear shirt and tie to every ministry activity, now casual wear has become the accepted norm not realizing to where this mindset is leading.

I've heard every excuse as to why we need to dress down, but what many don't realize is this a mindset is a direction that is being engrained in our youth. The problem with this change is that once you start changing, you will never stop moving. If you don't believe me, just look at how many young ladies dress in churches today. Years ago their mothers would have never let them go to church dressed in the attire they are today, but it all started with dressing down. It is so bad today that in many churches the preacher has to look at the back wall to keep a pure mind as indecent young ladies show their thighs off while they sit on the front row.

I know that this chapter will be one of the least popular and most criticized chapters in this book, but the dressing down mindset is leading to the eventual compromise of churches and immorality between couples and youth. The mind is corrupt enough without giving the flesh opportunity to lust and compromise. There are several dangers connected with this mindset and direction to dress down about which we must be careful. Let me share with you these dangers.

1. It destroys the importance of church.

Church should always be an important event. It should always be expected to dress up for church instead of dressing down. Ecclesiastes 9:10 reminds us, *"Whatsoever thy hand findeth to do, do it with thy might..."* If church is important, and it is, we should make sure we dress accordingly.

Romans 12:1-2 says, *"I beseech you therefore, brethren, by the mercies of God, that ye present your bodies a living sacrifice, holy, acceptable unto God, which is your reasonable service. And be not conformed to this world: but be ye transformed by the renewing of your mind, that ye may prove what is that good, and acceptable, and perfect, will of God."* The Scriptures are very clear that the believer is to do their best for God. Every argument I hear about dressing down has to do with making ourselves more appealing to the world. God says in the verse above not to *"be conformed to this world."* The believer shouldn't be trying to change their dress to appeal to the world, but they should be dressing to please their Saviour.

2. It shows the mindset a believer has towards Christ.

If the believer is willing to dress down for serving the LORD, it reveals that their respect for God is not what it should be. Matthew 22:37 says, *"Jesus said unto him, Thou shalt love the Lord thy God with all thy heart, and with all thy soul, and with all thy mind."* Anything the believer does for the LORD should be their best. When the believer dresses down for church, they are not giving the LORD their best, and it reveals their mindset that the LORD doesn't need the best.

3. It leads to immodest dressing.

A casual mindset always leads to immodesty. Look at the children of Israel when they danced around the golden calf; their casual mindset towards worshipping God led to their acceptance to dance naked. (Exodus 32:25) Immodesty always starts by dressing down. Nobody ever woke up one day and said that they were going to be immodest in their dress; but, immodesty is a result of the first step to choose to dress down. Every church that has lost its Christ-honoring dress standards lost them when they chose the dress-down mindset.

4. It leads towards immorality.

A dress-down mindset always leads to lack of respect for yourself and those around you. According to the Scriptures, the nakedness is the thigh. Isaiah 47:2 says, *"Take the millstones, and grind meal: uncover thy locks,* **make bare the leg, uncover the thigh***, pass over the rivers."* Notice that God shows the nakedness of a person is when they uncover their thigh.

Dressing down eventually leads to nakedness. I can see the modern day Balaam's, who have sold themselves to the world, rolling their eyes as I point out that dressing down leads to nakedness. However, any person knows that followers will often not live according to the standard of the leaders. If the leaders are willing to dress down, the followers will have lower standards for dress. This will only lead to one thing; indecency. When people become indecent, they will eventually commit immorality. Galatians 6:8 proves this when it says, *"For he that soweth to his flesh shall of the flesh reap corruption..."* You have a better chance of avoiding immorality if you continue to dress up for the things of the LORD.

5. Compromise is achieved through small moves.

One of the greatest dangers of dressing down is that you have moved from where you once stood. Satan never asks the believer to compromise immediately, but he only wants you to move from your present stance. Throughout the Scriptures, you find that Satan attempts to get the believer to move slowly. One of those times is when he tried to get Daniel and the three Hebrew children to eat the meat of the king. They knew that they shouldn't eat that meat because God strictly commanded the Hebrews not to eat the meat of the heathen. Satan didn't offer these Hebrews to stop serving God; he just asked them to move a little.

Satan's plan for the believer has never changed. He is always trying to get the believer to move a little at a time. If he can get the believer to stop dressing up for church, maybe he can get them to miss church the next time. If he can get the believer to dress down, maybe the next time he can get them to lower their dress standards. His eventual goal is for the believer to be indecent, so he offers to dress down knowing that one move always leads to another. Those who would argue against me need to look no further than the churches that accepted the dressing down mindset in the 70s and 80s and see how they dress today. You can say that dressing down doesn't matter, but you are falling for the age-old trick of Satan to get you to move just a little bit. He knows that if you will move a little now that He can get you to move more later.

6. Dressing down leads to a change of Christ-honoring dress standards.

There used to be a day when most churches believed that ladies should only wear dresses; however, the dress-down mentality has changed all of this. It doesn't matter that Deuteronomy 22:5 says, *"The woman shall not wear that which pertaineth unto a man, neither shall a man put on a woman's garment: for all that do so are abomination unto the LORD thy God."* It doesn't matter that God showed the standard in the priests dress that men wear pants when He says, *"And the priest shall put on his linen garment, and his linen breeches..."* (Leviticus 6:10) The fact is that when believers are willing to dress down to be accepted by the world, their ladies will eventually lower their Christ-honoring standard to wear pants.

Not only has it led to ladies leaving the Christ-honoring standard of dresses, but dressing down has led men to lower their Christ-honoring standards to wear bracelets and necklaces which are ladies' attire. My friend, whenever you choose to dress down, you are taking on a mindset that eventually lowers every Christ-honoring standard just so that you can appeal to the world.

7. Dressing down leads to purposeless living.

The word "casual" means, no design. A believer who accepts a casual mindset always lives their life with no design or principle. It was this mindset that led Israel to do *"that which was right in his own eyes."* (Judges 17:6) If the believer is going to please the LORD, they must live to fulfill the purpose of why He placed them on this Earth. The mindset of dressing down is a mindset to do less than our best. When you do less than your best, you will always find purpose of living for God will quickly become a purpose of appealing to the world.

8. Dressing down leads to a playing mindset instead of a worshipping mindset.

When the children of Israel accepted the dressing-down mindset, they also lost the mindset of proper worship. It is interesting that Moses said about these people in Exodus 32:18-19, *"… but the noise of them that sing do I hear. And it came to pass, as soon as he came nigh unto the camp, that he saw the calf, and the dancing…"* Their dressing down led to worldly music that didn't glorify the LORD and dancing around a golden calf.

It is no wonder that many of the churches today that have a dressing-down mindset also have worldly music. It is interesting that these same churches focus more on their rock concert style of music and dancing than they do the preaching of the Word of God. You will always see the preaching change in a church when it accepts the mindset to dress down. Dressing down always leads to worldly and fleshly mindset that accept things you once never used to accept in the church.

9. Dressing down leads to a loss of respect for each other.

When a person doesn't respect God enough to dress up, they will also lose respect for others. Matthew 22:37 commands the believer to love the LORD God with *"all thy heart, and with all thy soul, and with all thy mind."* Verse 39 follows up by saying, *"...Thou shalt love thy neighbour as thyself."* Your respect for others is directly connected with your respect for God. Dressing down shows your lack of respect for God, which results in a lack of respect for authorities and each other. A lack of respect for others always leads to doing sinful things with or against others that you normally would not do if you respected them; which is commonly immorality.

10. Dressing down eventually leads to casualties.

Before a person is ever a casualty, they will always be casual. Take the "ty" off casualty, and you have casual. If you don't want to become a casualty, you need to guard against becoming casual. Dressing down always leads to casual living. Dressing up for the LORD helps you to keep from accepting the casual mindset that has infiltrated our churches and has led to indecent dress, worldly living, and immorality.

My friend, I am not saying that men have to work in a shirt and tie, but I am saying that men should dress up when they serve the LORD. I am not saying that a lady has to do housework in her church attire, but I am saying that a lady should dress up for church. Always remember that whatever standard of dress you accept for church always leads to a lower standard of dress as you do your business around town. If you don't want to get to the point of indecency, it would be right to dress up for the LORD.

You can't argue with history. History has proven that dressing down always leads to indecent dress. The church and the believer should learn from history that we don't need to be conformed to the world, but we need to dress in a manner that shows our highest respect for God. Don't accept Satan's offer to move your standard for dress or Christ-honoring dress standards. Remember that if he can get you to move one time, he eventually will get you to move again. Stop accepting the offer to dress down, and show the LORD the respect He deserves by dressing up for every ministry activity that you do for Him.

Chapter 21

ACTIONS WITH NO CONSEQUENCES

Eighteen and a half seconds is truly what it took to blow the Watergate scandal wide open. It was not the initial crime that took President Nixon down, but it was the eighteen and a half seconds that he deleted from a recorded conversation that showed his involvement in trying to sabotage the Democratic Party. The Watergate scandal will always be the gold standard of coverups. President Nixon will always be associated with the Watergate scandal because of his choice to cover up the crime.

Coverups are often more detrimental than the crime that was committed. Many sports figures have lost their jobs because they attempted to cover up their actions instead of facing the consequences of those actions. Many people have tried to cover up their minor discrepancies in an attempt to save their reputation, only to find that the coverup is what became the major damage to their reputation. You cannot cover up sin and think that you are going to get away with it. When something wrong has been done, you must deal with it immediately and scripturally.

One of the things that has plagued churches for many years is that we don't deal with sin in a scriptural matter. Many who have done wrong had their sin swept under the carpet only to be revealed later. What is worse about these cover-ups is that these people continue to commit greater sin because there were no consequences for their actions. You cannot allow people to do wrong without paying the consequences for their actions.

One thing that every leader must be careful about is that they don't let their heart overtake how God says to deal with sin. Sin is bad enough, but when you don't deal with it properly, it will only get worse. Many preachers, in an attempt to salvage someone, has swept sin under the carpet only to see that person do worse afterward. We must be careful about building a culture of coverups because it only leads to people thinking that they can do wrong and continue to get away with it.

Sadly, many parents have made the same mistake of not dealing with the sin of their children because they don't want to hurt their feelings. What parents don't understand is if they don't deal with the sin of their children when it's small, it will only lead to greater sin when they become adults. The greater that sin becomes, the greater the consequences will be. The embarrassment of dealing with your child's sin now when it is smaller will be microcosmic compared to the hurt you will feel when they get caught doing something greater.

Actions without consequences is no way to deal with sin. If we want to remove sin from someone's life and see them go on to usefulness, we must be sure that their sin is dealt with scripturally and properly the first time they are caught. There are several dangers of covering up sin that we will regret if we don't deal with it properly. Let me share with you the consequences of covering up sin instead of dealing with it in a scriptural manner.

1. Covering sin emboldens the sinner to do more.

One of the reasons that sin must be dealt with properly is because you embolden the sinner when they get away with their wrong. Look at Eli's boys in 1 Samuel 2. Eli rebuked his boys, but they didn't listen. The rebuke was not enough because they knew their father wouldn't follow through by removing them from the priesthood. Eli's inability to deal with sin properly led to these boys committing adultery with women in the tabernacle. The boldness of these young men to commit sin in the tabernacle was a direct result of their sin being covered up.

You cannot allow sin to happen without consequences and think that those who sinned will miraculously stop doing wrong. Consequences always have a way of putting the brakes on sin. Whether it is a pastor, parent or leader, you must follow through with consequences if you want sin to stop. If you don't, your inaction emboldens the sinner to do greater sin until they are finally stopped by a greater power.

2. Covering sin leads to greater guilt.

When David committed adultery with Bathsheba, guilt gripped his heart because he didn't deal with it. The only way he knew how to deal with guilt was to attempt to cover it up by having Bathsheba's husband come home from the battle to sleep with his wife. The problem was that David's coverup plan didn't work when Uriah, instead of going inside to sleep with his wife, slept on the doorstep of his house. David's guilt led to the great plot to have Uriah killed.

You are not doing anyone a favor by covering sin. One of the reasons guilt is present when sin is covered is because the person who sinned knows they did wrong, and they are just waiting for someone to find out. Whenever you cover sin, you are allowing guilt to build in the heart of the fallen, which only leads to greater sin. The only way to get rid of a person's guilt is to come clean with what they have done. David realized this is Psalm 51, and after he came clean, he felt the freedom and sweet presence of God's Holy Spirit working in his life again. If you want to help a person overcome the guilt of sin, you must remove the sin that caused the guilt, and that will never be done by covering it up.

3. Covering sin from man doesn't cover it from God.

David thought he had gotten away with his sin, but God still knew about it. 2 Samuel 11:27 says, *"But the thing that David had done displeased the LORD."* David had successfully executed his plan to cover up his sin, but his attempt to cover it with man failed with God. God knew what David had done, and though he thought he got away with it, his sin still *"displeased the LORD."*

It really doesn't matter how successful you are in covering sin, it will one day be revealed. The one factor many people never consider is the God-factor. You may have enough power to cover your sins with man, but you will never be able to pull the wool over God's eyes. God sees everything you do, and He still holds those who commit sin accountable for their actions. Covering sin never takes God out of the situation.

4. The cover-up makes the consequences greater.

Look at how great David's consequences were for covering his sins. The baby who was born in sin died. His son, Amnon, raped his sister. Absalom killed his brother Amnon, and also led a coup attempt against his father. All of this happened because David didn't deal with his sin properly.

The coverup always causes the consequences to be greater. People will forgive you when you come clean, but they rarely forgive those who deceived them by covering up sin. Proverbs 28:13 says, *"He that covereth his sins shall not prosper: but whoso confesseth and forsaketh them shall have mercy."* My friend, you will create more enemies if you choose to cover sin. The anger that people will have for you will be great and hard to overcome because of the mistrust you created by covering up sin.

5. The covering of sin will eventually be torn away.

Numbers 32:23 says, *"…be sure your sin will find you out.* You can only hide sin for so long before God reveals it openly. One of the reasons you need to get right with the LORD immediately is so that your sins will not be exposed openly. You may have been successful in covering sin for a long time, but eventually, God will tear the cover away and the sin will become open to all. Many have suffered greater embarrassment and consequences than they would have had to suffer had they not covered up their sin. Don't fall into Satan's trap of thinking that you are different from others and that you have the ability to keep your sin covered. The God-factor is one area you are never able to overcome. Dealing with sin immediately and properly is always better than having to deal with the fallout that your coverup causes.

6. The purpose of consequences is to restore the fallen.

Why do we have consequences? The reason is because we need to restore the fallen. The fallen cannot start the process of restoration until the consequences of sin are set in place. Psalm 51 is a great example of how a fallen man saw God restore him because he finally dealt with his sin properly. God's mercies cannot be experienced until the fallen comes clean with their sin. Covering sin delays God's ability to exercise mercy. The best way to deal with sin is to come clean immediately so that God can grant mercy to the fallen.

With all of this in mind, how do we restore the fallen? Galatians 6 is the best answer to this question. In this chapter, God shows the proper way of dealing with sin so that you don't have to cover it up.

1. Deal with the sin to the degree of its openness.

The two best examples of dealing with sin are the woman at the well and the book of 1 Corinthians. The woman at the well was a sinner who had never been confronted with her sin until she met Jesus. Though her sin was great, it was not open to the world; thus, God dealt with her as an individual and she was able to make something of her life.

On the other hand, the church in Corinth covered their sin, even though everyone knew about it. Because they were so brazen about their sin, God had to deal with it openly. It wasn't the depth of the sin that caused God to have to deal with it openly, but it was how open these people were with their sin that caused it to be dealt with before the whole church.

You should always deal with sin to the degree of its openness. The purpose of having consequences is not to hurt the sinner, nor is it to show how hard you are on sin; rather, the purpose of consequences is for the sinner to know the pain sin caused so they will avoid greater sin later.

Let the degree of openness and the responsibility of the fallen dictate how open you must be in dealing with sin. I don't believe the Scriptures want us to bring all sin before the church to see, but I do believe when a person of responsibility has committed a sin worthy of their removal, it should be dealt with in an open manner. The person of responsibility knew better, and if you don't deal with it openly, it will cause many not to understand why they were removed. Again, I don't think it is everyone's business to know what a person has done, but people do need to know when a person who held a position of leadership did something that caused them to have to step down. 1 Timothy 5:20 makes this clear when it says, *"Them that sin rebuke before all, that others also may fear."*

2. Punish with usefulness in mind.

Galatians 6:1 says, *"Brethren, if a man be overtaken in a fault, ye which are spiritual, restore such an one..."* Notice that the purpose of dealing with sin was to restore the fallen. It is not hateful to punish sin, because restoration cannot be started until the punishment of sin has been handed down.

However, the whole reason you deal with the fallen is so that they can be restored to the point of usefulness.

3. Don't remove the consequences.

Forgiveness doesn't mean that there are no consequences. Many hold the mentality that a person never loses anything when they sin. Just because you say, "I'm sorry" doesn't mean you can get away without suffering the consequences. My friend, sin always causes you to forfeit something. The principle of sin's consequences can be seen in Galatians 6:7 when it says, *"Be not deceived; God is not mocked: for whatsoever a man soweth, that shall he also reap."*

I am not saying that you need to be hateful with the person who has done wrong, but they need to know that their sin caused them to lose some of the privileges they once had. David didn't get to go on with life as if nothing had happened; rather, God granted mercy as He dealt the punishment of sin. If a person has done something that has caused them to forfeit the right to ever hold a certain position again, be careful not to remove the consequences because of the closeness of the individual or their apology for their wrong. The consequences of sin still must be administered if you want to help restore the fallen back to usefulness.

4. Don't think you are above the fallen.

Galatians 6:1 continues by saying, *"...restore such an one in the spirit of meekness; considering thyself, lest thou also be tempted."* Be careful about acquiring a condescending attitude towards the fallen. The reason God allows you to help restore the fallen is because He believes you are spiritual enough to deal with them. God says in this verse, "...**ye which are spiritual**, *restore such an one...*" God gives the responsibility of restoring the fallen to a spiritual person. A spiritual person will deal in meekness when restoring the fallen. A spiritual person will always be careful about condemning because they know that they are capable of falling. You will never be successful in restoring the fallen if you are condescending and unspiritual. Always keep in mind that you are just as capable of doing the same sin when you are trying to restore someone back to usefulness.

5. Use God's Word to restore.

Galatians 6:6 says, *"Let him that is taught in the word communicate unto him that teacheth in all good things."* Only God's Word can restore the fallen. Psychology and philosophy have never restored the fallen; only God's Word restores them because it cleans them from the inside out. If you are going to be successful in bringing the fallen back to usefulness, you must throw man's philosophies aside and let the Scriptures guide the fallen back to God.

6. Expect setbacks, but don't quit.

Galatians 6:9 says, *"And let us not be weary in well doing: for in due season we shall reap, if we faint not."* God knew that the process of restoring the fallen would be wearisome, but you cannot give up on them. The fallen is going to have setbacks because sin has strengthened their flesh and weakened their spirit. Don't let their spiritual setbacks cause you to give up on them.

ACTIONS WITH NO CONSEQUENCES

My friend, there are consequences to sin. Be careful about removing the consequences because it only leads to greater sin and consequences down the road. If you deal with sin according to the Scriptures, you will find that you will keep others from falling and help more people to come back to usefulness.

CHAPTER 22

LEGACY DRIVEN SOCIETY

God told Saul to completely destroy the Amalekites. For whatever reason, Saul didn't take God's command seriously. When Saul and Israel went to war, they *"spared Agag, and the best of the sheep, and of the oxen, and of the fatlings, and the lambs, and all that was good, and would not utterly destroy them: but every thing that was vile and refuse, that they destroyed utterly."* (1 Samuel 15:9) The excuse they used was that they wanted to use the animals for sacrifice, but their actions were nothing more than rebellion.

When Saul was asked about these actions from Samuel, he said that they had completely obeyed the LORD. Though Saul thought he could hide what he did from the prophet, God had already told Samuel what Saul did. When Samuel told Saul that God had rejected him from being king, he turned himself to go away. As Samuel started walking away, Saul grabbed Samuel's mantle and tore it trying to keep the prophet from walking away without honoring him. When Samuel turned back, Saul said, *"...I have sinned: yet honour me now, I pray thee, before the elders of my people, and before Israel, and turn again with me, that I may worship the LORD thy God."* (1 Samuel 15:30)

It is very evident that Saul was more interested in his legacy being in place than he was with dealing with the rebellion in his heart. Saul started out right, but he fell into the same trap that many leaders fall into by trying to build a legacy for themselves. He wanted others to remember him for what he did instead of doing what he was supposed to do to obey the LORD.

The longer I live, the more I see that the political leaders of our day are more interested in building their legacy than they are about doing right for their country. One of the sad statements you hear at the end of a President's final term is how his final actions are all about building his legacy. What seems superficial to me is how every former President builds their library to brag about what they did as president. Though there is much history to be learned from these presidential libraries, I believe too many presidents have been more concerned with building their legacy than they have with what is best for their country. If America is ever going to be a great nation again, she will have to have a president who is not concerned with building his legacy but one who is concerned with doing what is best for his country.

Sadly, it seems that many preachers have fallen into the trap of legacy building more than they are about building the kingdom of God. I have watched many preachers who seem to be building their own kingdom so they can keep their name alive instead of doing what is best for the LORD. This legacy-driven society has led to pastor's covering sin, hiring their children to fill leadership roles that others should rightfully hold, and trying to impress people with their resumé and demand with speaking engagements. It seems that this legacy-driven society is more interested in buildings being named after them than they are with the cause of Christ and building the lives of those whom they are to lead.

This legacy-driven mentality is no different from Absalom who built a pillar for himself. 2 Samuel 18:18 says, *"Now Absalom in his lifetime had taken and reared up for himself a pillar, which is in the king's dale: for he said, I have no son to keep my name in remembrance: and he called the pillar after his own name: and it is called unto this day, Absalom's place."* Absalom was all about one person; himself. He wasn't concerned with the needs of the people; rather, he was concerned with what position he could hold so that he could build his legacy. This mindset led to a legacy, but not the type of legacy he wanted. It led to a legacy as the gold standard for rebellion. Whenever anyone talks about rebellion, they are often compared to Absalom. His desire to build a legacy for himself not only destroyed him, but it led many others down the same trail of death.

My friend, there are several reasons why you must avoid this legacy-driven mentality. The legacy-driven mentality always leads to destruction. There are eight dangers of a legacy-driven mentality.

1. A legacy-driven mentality is selfishness at its core.

At best, worrying about your legacy is a selfish motive. Absalom wanted a legacy so that he could be remembered. Saul wanted a legacy so that people would honor him. In both instances, these men were more concerned with what they got out of things instead of fulfilling the responsibilities of their positions.

2 Timothy 3:2 tells us that the last days will be filled with legacy-driven people when it says, *"For men shall be lovers*

of their own selves, covetous, boasters, proud…" No person should ever be so selfish that they are concerned with how they will be remembered. Philippians 2:4 tells us what builds the greatest legacy when it says, *"Look not every man on his own things, but every man also on the things of others."* The problem with trying to build one's own legacy is that one day they will be revealed for who they are. Proverbs 11:26 says, *"He that withholdeth corn, the people shall curse him: but blessing shall be upon the head of him that selleth it."* The selfishness of a legacy-driven individual will one day lead to people despising them for how they hurt others while trying to build their legacy.

2. A legacy-driven mentality leads to idolatry.

One of the biggest problems with legacy-driven people is that they lead their followers to measure truth by their leader's desires. One statement that I often hear people say is, "What will the preacher think of this?" The problem is that the preacher is not who we are supposed to be serving. However, many spiritual leaders make their ministry about themselves instead of about what the LORD wants. Some of the phrases you will hear from legacy-driven preachers are: "This is my church, and I will do what I want to do." "This is my world, and you will do what I tell you to do." These are dangerous statements because it should never be about what we want, but what Christ wants.

Paul made this very evident when he said, *"Be ye followers of me, even as I also am of Christ."* (1 Corinthians 11:1) God makes it clear who our example to follow is in 1 Peter 2:21 when He says, *"For even hereunto were ye called: because*

Christ also suffered for us, leaving us an example, that ye should follow his steps:" The legacy driven-leader will fall short of these examples because they make themselves the one to follow.

3. A legacy-driven mentality leads to compromise.

The problem with building your own legacy is that one day you will compromise that for what you once stood. The greatest example of this is Saul. Saul started out being the best man in Israel whom God described as *"a goodlier person."* Yet, because he was concerned with his legacy, he was willing to leave a heart to please God to a heart to please the people all so his legacy could continue.

When you become more concerned with what others think about you than what God thinks about you, you are held captive to the desires and whims of your followers. Truth no longer becomes your sole focus because you will do what you have to do to keep people looking to you. Thus, compromise sets in when what is right won't make you popular resulting in your legacy being destroyed. You cannot be a legacy builder and hold to the truth at the same time.

4. A legacy-driven mentality uses people to build a legacy.

One of the most dangerous traps any leader can fall into is using people to build their work instead of using their work to build people. Legacy-driven leaders use people until that person is no longer useful to building their legacy. When a person is no longer useful to them, they are often discarded and left to deal with the realization that they were used to build a man's legacy.

When you think about how to build a legacy, you should look no further than Christ. Philippians 2:7 says that He *"made himself of no reputation."* However, the legacy of Christ is found in Acts 10:38 when it says, *"...who went about doing good..."* Jesus didn't build a legacy by trying to build one, but He built a legacy by building people. Mark 10:28 confirms this when it says, *"For even the Son of man came not to be ministered unto, but to minister, and to give his life a ransom for many."* Those who use people to build their legacy will have a legacy, but not one by which they will want to be remembered. Great legacies are built by selfless living. Any leader who lives to build their legacy will find a soiled legacy that people will look at with disregard.

5. A legacy-driven mentality leads to abusive power.

Saul was out to build his legacy, and when David came in between him and his legacy, he tried to have him killed. The problem with having a legacy-driven mentality is that you will try to destroy anyone who interferes with your legacy.

1 Corinthians 9:18 warns of this when it says, *"What is my reward then? Verily that, when I preach the gospel, I may make the gospel of Christ without charge,* **that I abuse not my power** *in the gospel."* The legacy-driven mentality always uses its power to build itself instead of using its power to build people. If you don't want to leave a trail of abused Christians, you had better be sure you don't live to build your legacy. Many people have become bitter at Christianity

because they were part of a ministry where the leader used his power to build his legacy. Though bitterness of an abused follower is never right, a leader should never abuse their power to ensure that their legacy stays intact.

6. A legacy-driven mentality leads to interpreting truth according to your legacy.

Absalom is a great example of how a legacy-driven mentality skews your view of truth. Absalom felt his father didn't treat people right, and he felt that his father didn't handle situations right. Why did he think this? He thought this because he was trying to build his legacy. His legacy-driven mentality led him to believe that he was the one who was always right, yet the Scriptures reveal that he wasn't the one who was right.

Truth will always be skewed by the legacy-driven individual. The legacy-driven individual looks at truth through the prism of their legacy, and that is how they justify doing wrong. The danger of a legacy-driven mentality is that it causes an individual to see wrong as right and right as wrong depending on how it affects their legacy.

7. A legacy-driven mentality leads to a lost focus of purpose.

At the end of Hezekiah's life, he acquired a legacy-driven mentality. Hezekiah became so proud of all that he had done that he exposed the palace to the enemy. When confronted with this foolish act and that his children would become servants to the enemy he said, *"...Is it not good, if peace and truth be in my days?"* (2 Kings 20:19)

Hezekiah lost total focus of his purpose because he was being controlled by the legacy-driven mentality. He didn't care that others would be hurt and die because he felt his legacy would stay intact while he was alive.

The legacy-driven individual quickly loses focus of what they are supposed to be doing. They will find themselves happy that their legacy is built, even if it means that others will have to be hurt for that to happen. The legacy-driven mentality always causes you to lose focus that you are to live for Christ and others and not for yourself.

8. A legacy-driven mentality leads to kingdom building instead of Kingdom building.

The biggest problem with trying to build a legacy is that the individual lives their life trying to build their kingdom instead of trying to build the kingdom of God. The Scriptures make it clear that the purpose of the believer is to build the kingdom of God. Matthew 6:33 says, *"But seek ye first the kingdom of God, and his righteousness; and all these things shall be added unto you."* The believer's responsibility is to build one kingdom; God's.

The legacy-driven pastor will be more concerned with their kingdom than God's. This will keep churches from being started because the legacy-driven pastor is more concerned with how big their ministry is than they are with building the kingdom of God by reaching the world.

My friend, we will never reach this world with the Gospel with a legacy-driven mentality. If this world is going to be reached with the Gospel, we must stop worrying about our legacy and give our lives to building the kingdom of God. Your legacy will take care of itself when you live selflessly by reaching the lost for Christ, building lives, and spreading the Gospel around the world. When you look at those whose legacies have lived beyond their lifetime, you will find that they were not concerned with their legacy; instead, they lived their lives trying to please the LORD by building His kingdom. It is the selfless mentality of trying to build the kingdom of God that will determine what your legacy will become.

CHAPTER 23

REDEFINING ROLE MODELS

Throughout my lifetime, the role models which young people have followed has drastically changed. When I was a boy, it was not uncommon for boys to look up to firemen and policemen as their role models. It was not uncommon for parents to point their children to men of God and tell them to get their signatures in their Bible. Because parents pointed their boys to the preacher as a role model, many young men grew up with a desire to become a preacher.

It seems as though time has progressed to the point where role models have turned from public servants and preachers to Hollywood stars, sports figures, and worldly musicians. It is sad when young people want to be more like a pop star than they do a police officer, fireman, or preacher. It is sad to see a younger generation listening to sports figures and Hollywood stars who live immoral lives more than they do their parents. We live in a generation that is pointing to the wrong role models and it is destroying our youth. Satan knows that the way to destroy a society is by pointing the youth to the wrong role models.

Sadly, the mentality of pointing youth to the wrong role models has passed into our fundamental Baptist movement. It was common for years to point youth to men of God, parents, and spiritual authorities as role models to follow. There was a time when preachers were the heroes and not the villain. It was not uncommon for teenagers to line up after a service to get the signature of the man of God, or just want to spend time being around him.

We live in times when youth are being pointed to the wrong role models, which is resulting in them looking more like the world than they are servants of Jesus Christ. For whatever reason, preachers are preaching against youth looking to the preacher, but they don't mind when the same youth are looking to sports figures as heroes. It is sad when the supposed Christian sports figure is a greater hero than the man of God who invests his life in others. It is a travesty when the Christian schoolteacher who sacrifices to give the youth a good education is not as revered as the modern day comedian. It is a sin when parents are no longer considered the greatest heroes in a child's life but are considered out-of-touch with their children.

Let me ask you, what has the sports figure done for anyone? When is the last time a worldly musician showed up to help someone through a difficult time? When is the last time a Hollywood star was there for someone to cry on their shoulder?

It is amazing how those who sacrifice time with their family are no longer the role models we push our youth to admire. I am not talking at all about worshipping a man, but I do believe every person needs good role models to follow. Whether or not we like it, everyone is going to have a role model to follow. The best thing we could do is point them to the right role models to follow. We should be pointing our youth to those role models who will encourage them to serve the LORD with their lives.

Maybe the reason we don't point our youth to the proper role models is because we don't want them to serve the LORD full-time. We would rather our young people become business leaders than preachers. We would rather our young girls marry a successful businessman than we would for them to marry a preacher or missionary who is going to start a church in a storefront somewhere around the world.

This movement to redefine the role models is pushing our young people to the wrong standards. It is no wonder that young people are growing up despising church. The reason is because we have taken their attention away from the spiritual role models, and instead have allowed them to have worldly role models, which is resulting in the youth going to the world. I believe the enrollment in Bible colleges has decreased because we have pointed the younger generation to the wrong role models. One of the ways we are going to get young people to go into the ministry is by pointing them to the right role models so that they have a positive and spiritual influence to follow.

Sadly, pushing the wrong role models has also passed into the ministry. Many influential preachers today seem to be pointing younger preachers to the wrong role models, instead of pointing them to those who have given their lives for the old-paths, independent-Baptist movement. We have preachers today who promote the books of Bible compromisers and liberals over the books of old paths, Baptist preachers of the past who built large independent Baptist churches through separation, soul winning, and preaching. Today, it seems that the more worldly of a lifestyle that a preacher allows, the more he is held up as a role model to follow. We have more preachers identifying with modern day Balaam's than they are with preachers who stand for the old paths. You can look no further than social media to see many millennial preachers who are more enamored with the liberal preacher than they are with the old paths preacher.

My question to you is this; why are we so afraid to point to the heroes of the past who stood for and defended the old paths? Why are we afraid to embrace Jack Hyles, Lee Roberson, Tom Malone, J. Frank Norris and men like this who stood for the old paths and promoted holy living, old-time music, and ran buses to reach the lost for Jesus Christ as role models? Why is it that we are looking to worldly, spiritual gurus who pattern their lives after the flesh more than they do after the Word of God for ideas to grow our churches?

If we are not careful, we will destroy a whole generation of young preachers by pointing them to the wrong role models. Just look at the books being promoted by many of the independent, Baptist preachers. Let me ask you, why promote the books of men who don't believe the King James Bible is the inspired and preserved Word of God? Why promote the books of men who are not a Baptist? Why promote the books of individuals who don't believe in scriptural separation, holiness, and Christ-honoring standards?

Why is it that we are pointing to the wrong role model? Why discourage the youth from looking to those spiritual leaders who walk the ways of the LORD and live according to the Word of God? Why point to people who don't believe in the King James Bible?

The Scriptures are very clear about pointing to the right role models. God tells us in 2 Thessalonians 2:15, *"Therefore, brethren, stand fast, and hold the traditions which ye have been taught, whether by word, or our epistle."* It is interesting that God is very interested in pointing to the right role models. God says that the role models to which we should point should be those who hold the traditions *"which ye have been taught, whether by word, or our epistle."*

2 Thessalonians 3:6-7 says, *"Now we command you, brethren, in the name of our Lord Jesus Christ, that ye withdraw yourselves from every brother that walketh disorderly, and not after the tradition which he received of us. For yourselves know how ye ought to follow us: for we behaved not ourselves disorderly among you;"* These verses give scriptural principles about pointing to the proper role models.

1. There are brothers in Christ from whom we will have to separate.

Notice that God says, *"...withdraw yourselves from every brother that walketh disorderly..."* This verse is not talking about withdrawing from the world, but it is talking about the necessity to withdraw from those who claim to be Christians but do not walk according to the traditions and principles which we have received from men of God from the past. It is scriptural to withdraw yourself from those who do not live according to that which we have been taught.

2. It is scriptural to have godly role models.

Verse 7 says, *"For yourselves know how ye ought to follow us: for we behaved not ourselves disorderly among you;"* There is nothing wrong with pointing people to the right role models. In fact, Paul commanded the Thessalonian believers to follow him because he was walking according to the traditions which had been given him. People are going to have role models in their lives, and they will fill that place in their life with someone. It is better to follow the Scriptures by pointing them to the right role models who obey the Word of God and follow the traditions and principles that were handed to us from previous generations than it is for them to follow a godless or compromising individual. If you discourage people from having scriptural role models, they will fill the need for role models with worldly ones.

3. Withdraw from influences who don't believe the King James Bible is the Word of God.

2 Thessalonians 2:15 says to stand fast with those who hold the traditions that have been taught *"by word, or our epistle."* In other words, standing fast with those who teach the Word means to withdraw from those who don't believe the King James Bible is the Word of God. In other words, don't follow preachers who won't take a strong stand for the King James Bible. Don't go to their churches, read their books, or associate with them by attending their conferences. They are a disorderly influence who could pull you away from what God wants you to be. A person who will not hold true to God's Word cannot be trusted as a good role model from which to glean truth. In fact, if you choose to follow and read

after those who don't use the King James Bible, you are rebelling against God and His Word.

4. Withdraw from those who don't hold the traditions taught by our forefathers.

It is interesting that God wants us to know what those before us taught. Sadly, there are people who avoid being associated with those preachers from the past who stood strongly for the old paths. God makes it clear that you are to withdraw yourself from those who won't identify with the old paths preachers from the past. 2 Thessalonians 3:6 says, *"…withdraw yourselves from every brother that walketh disorderly, and not after the tradition which he received of us."* There are men like J. Frank Norris, Jack Hyles, Tom Malone, and Lee Roberson who have shown us how to build a church without compromising the Word of God. These men from the past ought to be the role models to which we look to for ideas rather than the modern progressive preacher.

God makes it clear to withdraw or separate from those who criticize these types of men from the past. In other words, you should not go to old paths' critics for ideas, nor should you make them your role model or point others to their books or conferences. Any preacher or spiritual leader who would point you to anyone who doesn't hold true to the King James Bible should never be held in esteem as a role model to follow.

It is important to have the proper role models to follow. Let me challenge you to pull away from the wrong role models. Let me encourage you to point the youth to the type of role model that isn't ashamed of the King James Bible, running buses, has Christ-honoring standards, and will never criticize the preachers from the past.

There is nothing wrong with preachers being very clear that we do not pattern our ministries, nor do we gather ideas from men who don't believe like us. The mentality that we can take in the good and spit out the bones has never worked. I promise you, every time I hear someone make this statement, it is not long before I see them choking on the very bones of compromise that they said they could spit out. Many men have tried to read the books of liberals without the wrong influencing them, but the problem is it always influences them. You can't soak in the poison of their compromising doctrine without it eventually become a part of your mindset and actions.

Let me encourage you to make those you read after those who follow the men from the past, hold true to the old paths, believe in the King James Bible, have Christ-honoring standards, and who practiced personal soul winning. Don't let the Devil influence you to throw out those preachers who ran buses to pick people up for church, and preached the old paths with fire and passion. Make these type of men the heroes to which you point.

Let the warning from 2 Thessalonians be your admonition to withdraw from these brothers in Christ who don't hold true to the old paths. Certainly, these men may be saved, but there are times when you have to withdrawal from those who don't walk according to the old paths that were shown to us from the saints of old.

CHAPTER 24

THE DEVALUATION OF LIFE
THE TURNING POINT IN AMERICAN MORALITY

January 22, 1973, became the turning point in American morality. This was the day when abortion was legalized in America. This was the day when the Supreme Court legalized the murdering of a baby in the mother's womb in its *Roe v. Wade* ruling. Since that ruling, the devaluation of life and American morality has been on a downward spiral, and it is quickly going to depths that we would never imagine.

It is sad that we live in times when babies are considered tissue and not life. We live in times when euthanasia is considered compassionate for those who are suffering in life. We live in times when suicide is considered a moral decision when it comes to ending the life of an individual who deems they don't want to live because of "health issues." We live in times when doctors who are sworn to preserve life assist in patient suicide.

With all the shootings across America, many wonder how America has gone to such depths where individuals kill innocent people without hesitation. Many have wondered how a deranged man could shoot from a hotel tower in Las Vegas and kill so many innocent people? How is it that individuals take no thought about going into a school and shooting innocent children? How is it that an individual can walk into a church and shoot the parishioners, and then walk away as if nothing happened? How is it that American morality has dipped so low?

My answer to these questions is that this all started when the Supreme Court justices devalued the life of a baby by legalizing murder in the womb of the mother. This decision became the turning point of American morality. When a society no longer values life, it will begin an immoral downward spiral, and eventually become so degradative that politicians feel they have the right to determine who should and should not live.

We live in dark days. We live in days when politicians believe it is moral to kill a baby in the ninth month of pregnancy when the baby will inconvenience the mother. We live in days when a woman's choice is the reason its legal to kill a baby. What is not discussed is that the woman had a choice not to get pregnant, but her immoral life with an immoral man is what led to this pregnancy.

This is not the first time a society has ever dipped so low. Throughout history there were people who devalued life. Pharaoh was the first person recorded in history who devalued the life of a baby. Exodus 1:22 says, *"And Pharaoh charged all his people, saying, Every son that is born ye shall cast into the river, and every daughter ye shall save alive."* Pharaoh considered the Jews a threat to his power and the only way he believed he could stop this was to kill all the male babies at birth. Fortunately for Israel, there were nurses who feared God and felt that it was more important to keep a baby alive than it was to obey the command of Pharaoh to kill the male babies.

The devaluation of life took great strides when Charles Darwin promoted his godless philosophy of the survival of the fittest. He declared in his godless mentality that some races were more superior than others. It was this mentality that many dictators embraced to kill races they thought were inferior.

One of those dictators was Hitler. Hitler and the Nazi's totally embraced the humanistic, Darwinian thought of the supreme race. It was the embracing of this thought that caused them to feel it was morally acceptable to kill over six million Jews.

The devaluation of life is certainly seen in this present day when racial tensions are extremely high because politicians deem it productive for their cause to use skin color to divide people. The devaluation of life is seen in cities that have greater casualties than war zones, and the political leaders of the city do nothing to stop it. These things would not be if life were truly valued.

What is it that has caused our nation to dip so low that the life of an individual is not important? My answer to this question is that when you remove God from society, evil moves in. The Scripture says, *"Blessed is the nation whose God is the LORD..."* (Psalm 33:12) The reason American morality continues to take a dive is because we continue to push God out of our society, workplaces, politics, and public schools. We have become a society where morality is no longer an issue because God is no longer a part of the lives of Americans.

When you push God out, you will push out the value of life. The presence of God in a society helps people to realize that life is valuable because it is a gift from God. Genesis 2:7 teaches that God is the life-giver when it says, *"And the LORD God formed man of the dust of the ground, and breathed into his nostrils the breath of life; and man became a living soul."* It is the presence of God in a society that helps people to embrace the value of life.

When God is pushed out, morality will no longer be embraced. When God is pushed out, it becomes normal for teenagers to think nothing of committing fornication. When God is pushed out, adultery becomes an accepted lifestyle. When God is pushed out, you will have a society that stays out of churches on Sundays and Wednesdays. When God is pushed out, you will find a society that will accept immorality as moral, and morality as immoral.

It is sad that society has influenced the mindset of churches to the point where they struggle with whether it is right for sodomites to get married. Society has so influenced churches that some even struggle with whether or not abortion is truly murder. The churches of America, and I used the word "churches" very lightly, have lowered their standards so low that they have become nothing more than social clubs that promote immorality when they are supposed to be a place where holiness is expected, and God is lifted up.

What is the answer to turning this around? The answer is to bring God back into society. You will never bring a society back to God and morality until you bring back the value of life. Again, the turning point of American morality was when we legalized baby killing for a woman's choice. Throughout the Scriptures, God shows that life happens at conception when He says that a lady is *"with child."* If we don't get back to realizing that life begins at conception, the immoral downward spiral of our society will continue.

We must get back to realizing the importance of life; but how do we get back to this realization? The way that we will do this is by realizing the importance of each soul. My friend there is a real Heaven and Hell. If we don't realize that inside of every person is a soul that either goes to Heaven or Hell, we will continue to lose the importance of life. It is the soul of an individual that makes life so important.

The one thing that keeps the believer so focused on the importance of life is that we believe there is a soul. The thing that makes the believer different from others is that we believe *"man became a living soul."* (Genesis 2:7) The reason we believe that human life is of more value than animal life is because we realize that inside of every person is a soul that will spend an eternity in either Heaven or Hell.

My friend, I want you to understand that the only way we can turn the downward spiral of immorality around in our nation is for you to become a soul winner for Jesus Christ. We can only remove immorality from the heart by the saving grace of Jesus Christ. If the believer is not a personal soul winner, people will never discover the payment for their sins. It is the personal soul winner who shows the sinner there is hope through Jesus Christ.

There is one way to turn the immorality of our nation around. There is one way to make life valuable again. That way is to realize the value of each soul. I ask you this question; how valuable is a soul to you? Do you truly believe that each soul goes to Heaven or Hell? If you do, your soul winning life will show it. If you do, you will spend every week of your life telling every soul that there is a real Heaven they can go to if they will put their faith and trust in Jesus Christ to be their Saviour. This is the answer to turning around the downward spiral of immorality.

Let me encourage you to become a part of the solution for our society by making life valuable again. No, we won't make life valuable by holding hands around a city and showing our disdain for abortion; though I think it is good for believers to show their disagreement with abortion. We won't turn the downward spiral around by getting involved in politics; though I believe that those who hold political office are important to rewriting these immoral laws. I believe that the way we turn around this downward spiral of immorality is by valuing the soul of man. We will turn this spiral around by reaching every soul with the Gospel of Jesus Christ.

Are you going to be a part of the solution of turning the value of life around by reaching every soul? Or, are you going to sit idly by and let the devaluation of life and morality to continue to spiral downward because you never attempt to reach lost souls for Jesus Christ? America will see a revival of morality and life again when the soul of every American is reached with the Gospel.

CHAPTER 25

DISTRACTION
THE DEVIL'S TOOL TO DESTROY

Distraction is often the liberal's tactic for destroying good. Often a liberal tries to distract people away from their real actions so they can implement their destructive changes without anyone noticing. They use distraction as the diversion to get you off focus while they are destroying the very thing for which you stand. Todays liberal often creates false narratives to divert our attention away from what they are doing to destroy the foundational principles of America.

America has fallen for this diversion tactic, and it has destroyed the very core of our nation. The liberal has methodically chipped away at the core beliefs of the American soul to quickly turn us into a godless nation. They have accomplished this through the Satanic tool of distraction.

Satan has always used the tool of distraction to destroy God's institutions and causes. Satan desires to destroy every marriage and church because these are the two institutions God started. Satan has destroyed many marriages by getting a spouse to focus on a personal whim instead of staying focused on what they both have in common. Instead of focusing on the love for each other, Satan gets a spouse to focus on how their spouse is not doing something they like, which leads to problems in the marriage.

This same distraction tactic has been used to destroy many good independent Baptist churches. Satan has destroyed the spirit of many churches by distracting the members with personalities, conflicts and preferences instead of staying focused on God's Word and the Great Commission.

This distraction tactic started in the Garden of Eden. In Genesis 3:1 the Scripture says, *"Now the serpent was more subtil than any beast of the field which the LORD God had made. And he said unto the woman, Yea, hath God said, Ye shall not eat of every tree of the garden?"* You can see in this verse that Satan diverted Eve's attention from God's actual command. He got her to question what God actually said which diverted her attention away from God's original command. He masterfully used distraction by using a serpent to speak her. The serpent beguiled her and got her to get away from her purpose in the Garden. Eve's distraction eventually led to eating and giving the fruit to her husband, which led to sin entering into the world.

Satan's goal is not always getting the believer to fall into deep sin. He simply wants to get you not to do what God wants you to do. If he can distract the preacher from preaching the Gospel of Jesus Christ, he will use whatever distraction he can to keep him from preaching. If he can distract the believer from working on a bus route, going soul winning, or teaching a Sunday school class, he will use whatever diversion he can to distract them from doing what they are supposed to do. The Devil distracts the believer into focusing on something that they feel is more important, but in reality it is not uncommon for the distraction to be of lesser importance than the actual command that God wants the believer to obey.

You must be careful that distraction does not pull you away from what you are supposed to be doing. The Devil knows that if he can distract you from doing what you are supposed to do that he will eventually lead you down the road towards sin. There are four ways that the Devil distracts the believer from doing what they are supposed to do.

1. He distracts the believer through questions.

In Genesis 3, Satan asked Eve if God really said that she couldn't eat of every tree. Satan knew that once she questioned Scripture that he would be able to get her to change what God actually said. You have to be careful about being distracted by the questioning of those who are only trying to keep you from doing what you are supposed to do. The purpose of their questioning is to distract you from what you are supposed to do. If you spend time answering all their questions, you will stop doing what you are supposed to do. My friend, you have to realize that they are not questioning your beliefs because they desire to change, they are questioning your beliefs because they want to distract you from serving the LORD.

Always remember that it is not the believer's job to question God; it is the believer's job to obey Him. You must be careful that you don't allow the questions of those attacking the doctrines of the Scriptures to cause you to leave the very things that you believe. Just because they are questioning your beliefs doesn't mean you have to answer them. Proverbs 26:4 says, *"Answer not a fool according to his folly, lest thou also be like unto him."*

2. Satan distracts through diversion.

It is interesting that Satan got Eve to notice the one tree whose fruit she couldn't eat. Instead of looking at every other tree in the world that God gave her to eat of, she fell for Satan's trap to look at the one thing God wouldn't allow her to do.

Many Christians fall for this distraction by diversion. Instead of looking at everything God allows them to do, they focus on the one thing He tells them that they cannot do. We find this distraction is very common among teenagers, but many adults have also fallen for the same diversion. It is always amazing how there are those who get upset about what they cannot do, but they never notice all that they can do.

You will find many backslidden believers focus on the Christ-honoring standards of holiness when those Christ-honoring standards truly give the believer much freedom as to what they can still wear. Don't fall for Satan's diversion tactic. He's trying to get you to question one small thing to cause you to get bitter when you've got a whole world that you can enjoy. Adam and Eve were only told they couldn't eat of one tree, and they focused on the one tree they could not have instead of seeing the blessing of all the trees that God gave them to enjoy.

Watch out for Satan's diversion tactics. Be careful to understand that God gives you many more things to enjoy and do compared to every one thing that He tells you not to do. Don't let your focus get diverted by dwelling on what you cannot have and do. Don't get so diverted on what you don't like about God's standards for holiness that you miss the blessings that those standards bring.

For instance, many believers can get focused on one disagreement they have with God and how He handled a situation. Be careful that you don't become diverted over one disagreement with God when you agree with Him on one thousand other things. God is always right whether or not you agree with Him, but you cannot let Satan's diversion tactic cause you to focus on that one disagreement with God which causes you to pull you away from serving the LORD with all of your heart, soul and mind.

3. Satan distracts through worthy causes.

King Josiah got diverted by a worthy cause that eventually took him away from what he was supposed to be doing. Josiah got distracted by worrying about how the other nations were being ruled, and that diversion eventually led to his death.

Many believers get distracted by something that is a worthy cause, but it is not a cause worth taking them away from what they are supposed to be doing for the LORD. Preachers must be careful that they don't get caught up in worthy causes that pull them away from their calling. I have watched many preachers get distracted with their concern for what is going on in their nation. That concern for their nation led them to get caught up in politics which distracted them from fulfilling their calling. It is easy to become distracted and to let worthy causes to divert us away from our responsibilities, but you must not fall for this distraction by diversion.

There are many worthy causes you can get caught up in, but they are not worthy enough to pull you away from what God has called you to do. The greatest thing a preacher or a believer could do is to fulfill God's calling for their life. Any other calling is a distraction and is not worthy of your efforts.

4. Satan distracts with the peripheral.

If you were to ask the average pastor what he feels is the most important thing to do as a pastor, he would always say it is to study the Scriptures, spend time in prayer, and to go soul winning. Yet, when you ask the average pastor what he spends more time doing, you always find he spends more time in the office and the administrative duties of the church than he does in studying the Scriptures, praying or reaching the lost for Jesus Christ.

It's easy to become distracted with peripheral things. Be careful that you don't get distracted by things that will demand your attention, but really are not worthy of your attention. Nehemiah's response to this distraction is the response every believer should have with distractions. He said in Nehemiah 6:3, *"And I sent messengers unto them, saying, I am doing a great work, so that I cannot come down: why should the work cease, whilst I leave it, and come down to you?"* He realized the cause of building God's wall was greater than the opportunity to discuss differences with the enemy.

Don't get distracted in the peripheral battles. Stay focused on walking with the LORD, studying the Scriptures, prayer, and on leading people to Jesus Christ. Stay focused on building the lives of those whom God has given you to influence. Always remember that every minute that you are distracted is a minute you could have used doing God's will.

Satan always throws a big smoke ball to distract you from what you are supposed to be doing. If you stay focused on what the Scriptures tell you to do, you will be able to repeat the words of the Apostle Paul when he said, *"I have fought a good fight, I have finished my course, I have kept the faith:"* (2 Timothy 4:7)

Chapter 26

IF MY PEOPLE

We can get to the point when we look at everything that is happening and become discouraged about the prognosis of our country and the independent, fundamental Baptist movement. My answer to the concerns of those who are wondering what does our future hold is 2 Chronicles 7:14. This verse says, *"If my people, which are called by my name, shall humble themselves, and pray, and seek my face, and turn from their wicked ways; then will I hear from heaven, and will forgive their sin, and will heal their land."*

The hope for America winning against the attacks of political correctness is if God's people will choose to humble themselves and serve Him. The way to change a nation is always up to the individual. America will only be changed if you change. America will only do right if you do right. America will only serve the LORD if you serve the LORD.

The reason I make these statements is because you are America. America is a compilation of individuals. This means the hope of your nation being changed lies in your choice to do right. The hope of any nation is when the believers of that nation chooses as an individual to serve the LORD.

It is no question that the hope of a nation is in the believer doing right. Psalm 33:12 says, *"Blessed is the nation whose God is the LORD; and the people whom he hath chosen for his own inheritance."* The only way God is going to be the LORD of America is if you make God the LORD of your life.

I'm not talking about salvation with this statement, but I'm talking about making God that sole and supreme focus of Whom you serve. You will never change the world if you don't change your world. There are three worlds you must change if the world is going to change.

1. You must change your personal world.

You will never change the world until you decide to do right in the world of your personal life. It is the world of your personal life that determines the influence you will have in the world around you. Far too many believers are worried about what everybody else is doing instead of correcting what they need to do.

If you have come to this point of the book, you have read thousands of words that show the problems America and churches are facing today. Yet, it truly comes down to you doing right if you are going to be able to influence the world outside of your personal life. It truly comes down to whether you as an individual are going to take responsibility for your personal world and do right. Are you going to quit your sin? Are you going to read the Scriptures daily? Are you going to walk with the LORD in prayer? Are you going to live by Christ-honoring standards? Are you going to fight the sin that is going on in your own life? Are you going to be a personal soul winner to reach the lost for Jesus Christ? It comes down to you taking personal responsibility for your personal world to be able to change the world around you. If you don't take care of your personal world, the other two worlds that I'm about ready to discuss will never be changed.

2. You must change your daily interaction world.

The daily interaction world consists of your family, workplace, and neighborhood. We all have a daily interaction world in which we live. The family we have is part of our daily interaction world. Our place of employment is a part of our daily interaction world. The neighborhood in which we live is a part of our daily interaction world. Those everyday people we talk to are a part of our daily interaction world. Your church friend, world friends, and your neighbors are all a part of your daily interaction world. My friend, you will never change the daily interaction world of family, friends, work partners, and neighbors if you don't first get your personal world right.

Once you get your personal world right, you need to start doing right with your family, neighbors, and people with whom you work. The daily interaction world needs to see you living right. I worked in the secular world early on in my life, and I learned that the best testimony I could establish with them was to work hard and to live for the LORD in spite of the atmosphere they created. I learned that I could have the greatest influence on my supervisors, bosses, and fellow employees by working hard. You will never change your work world if you don't have a testimony of working hard and doing right all the time.

Men, the best way you can change your world at home is to love your wife. The best way a wife can change her world is to love and submit to the leadership of her husband. The best way parents can change the world of their children is to bring them up in the nurture and admonition of the LORD.

The best way for children to change the world of their home is to obey and honor their parents. When you do right in your world, those around you see you living like a Christian, which gives you the best chance to influence them.

The best way you can influence your neighbors is to be a good neighbor. The best way you can influence your boss is to be the best worker. The best way you can influence the people in your church is to get involved in the church ministries both in spirit and in action.

3. You must change the uttermost world.

The uttermost world is the world beyond your reach. You will never reach the uttermost world unless you have a spiritual influence in your own world and daily interaction world. The only thing that has allowed me as an evangelist to be able to reach beyond my world is that I've been able to keep my personal and daily interaction worlds right. Keeping these worlds right has allowed me the influence to reach the uttermost world.

There is a real world out there that is lost and going to Hell. One way you can reach this world is if you support missions so that missionaries can reach the uttermost world that you cannot reach.

Moreover, you can reach the uttermost world by getting involved in the ministries of your church to reach your city for Jesus Christ. You can reach the uttermost world by getting involved in your church's soul-winning ministries, Sunday school, and especially the bus ministry. By getting involved in these ministries, you are reaching a world of people that you would never meet in your daily interaction world. Serving the LORD through the ministries of your local, independent Baptist church helps you to reach an uttermost world.

Furthermore, there is a need for young men who will surrender their lives to serve God as full-time servants to go out of their world to reach another world. We will never turn this world around if young people and adults won't surrender to serve the LORD full time.

It always comes down to the believer as an individual to change their worlds if the world is going to be changed. God always left revival up to the personal actions of the believer. Revival won't happen just because sinners get saved, though it will have an influence, but revival will happen when every individual believer gets right with the LORD and serves Him. If you are saved, it is up to you as an individual to take personal responsibility to change your personal and daily interaction world before the uttermost world is changed. If you make sure your world is right, you will find that the daily interaction and uttermost worlds will be changed.

I'm glad that you've read the pages of this book, but let me challenge you to start making the needed changes in your world. The best way to fight the battles discussed in this book is for you to do right in your personal and daily interaction worlds. When you get those two worlds right, God can use you to influence the uttermost world. The answer has always been for the believer to do right, and for the local, independent Baptist church to stay focused on reaching the world with the Great Commission. This my friend, is the answer to winning this battle.

www.ingramcontent.com/pod-product-compliance
Lightning Source LLC
LaVergne TN
LVHW051549070426
835507LV00021B/2489